HunTers
OF THE AFRICAN SKY

Graeme Arnott

Peter Steyn
Graeme Arnott
Hunters
OF THE AFRICAN SKY

STRUIK
WINCHESTER

To the memory of

Leslie Brown (1917-1980)
and David Reid-Henry (1919-1977)

who shared our admiration for the
hunters of the African sky

STRUIK,
WINCHESTER,

An operating division of
The Struik Group (Pty) Ltd
Struik House, Oswald Pirow Street
Foreshore, Cape Town 8001
Registration number 80/02842/07

First published 1990

Edited by John Comrie-Greig
Designed by Wim Reinders & Associates cc, Cape Town
Dustjacket designed by Abdul Amien, Cape Town

Typesetting by McManus Bros (Pty) Ltd, Cape Town
Reproduction by Unifoto (Pty) Ltd, Cape Town
Printed in Singapore
Sponsors' and Collectors' Editions bound by Peter Carstens, Johannesburg
Standard Edition bound in Singapore

The Sponsors' Edition is limited to 26 copies, lettered from A to Z.
The Collectors' Edition is limited to 150 copies, numbered from 1 to 150.
The Standard Edition comprises 4 000 unnumbered copies.

ISBN 0 947430 19 9 (Sponsors' Edition)
ISBN 0 947430 18 0 (Collectors' Edition)
ISBN 0 947430 17 2 (Standard Edition)

CONTENTS

ARTIST'S ACKNOWLEDGEMENTS

It is now fifteen years since Peter Steyn and I planned and started work on the plates for *Birds of Prey of Southern Africa*. In this book these plates have been supplemented by ten new "scenic" plates and several working drawings. It has been a great pleasure to be inspanned alongside Peter once again. His infectious enthusiasm and meticulous efficiency have done wonders to encourage the artwork, while his provision of photographs for reference on almost all species represented has been invaluable. I have been able to complete the plates confident in the knowledge that the text could be in no better hands.

Some years ago I spent a memorable and exciting evening in the company of John Carlyon and Penny Meakin when they photographed the rare eastern Cape subspecies of the Barred Owl – a notable first. More recently I joined them in the Drakensberg, this time observing and drawing Bearded and Cape Vultures, Black Eagles and Jackal Buzzards while they photographed. They have kindly given me access to all their photographic material for use as reference. I am indebted to Ray Black for reference photographs of a Taita Falcon that he had nursed back to health in Zimbabwe.

Alan Kemp has always been a source of encouragement and has rendered us all a great service by making the inspiring work of Claude Gibney Finch-Davies available to the general public. He has also contributed a generous Foreword to our book.

Pieter Struik, our publisher, has been enthusiastic about this book from its earliest stages, and his encouragement and attention to quality have made our task a pleasant one.

FOREWORD

What is the best way to conserve a natural resource such as the birds of prey that fill our skies and kill, like us, other animals for their food? We can make extensive studies to determine how the birds live and what factors affect them, we can go to great lengths to shield them and their nest-sites from interference, or we can enact strict laws to protect them. However, none of these efforts is likely to be effective unless the populace has such an appreciation of birds of prey that they really want to conserve them.

Peter Steyn and Graeme Arnott have already made a major contribution to our understanding of the resource with their 1982 book *Birds of Prey of Southern Africa*. In this work Peter documented in detail the biology of all 80 species in the subcontinent, including many details from his own studies and his fine photographs of nests and young. Graeme provided masterly identification plates of all species in their various plumages, at rest and in flight. This work received the wide acclaim it deserved, offers still the most readable account for the raptor fauna of any region of the world, and hence is already into its third impression. Now they have switched the emphasis. Graeme's artistic mastery has been used as the vehicle to encourage an awareness of the spectacle, variety and beauty offered by the birds of prey of southern Africa. The colour identification plates from the earlier book have been enhanced to serve not only illustrative but also aesthetic ends and additional plates, of individual species in their natural settings, have been included. This sensitive and accurate artwork, complemented by Peter's brief text, full of insight, interest and accuracy, must catch the attention of many who were not previously aware of what a rich avian resource graces the subcontinent. The net result should be many more people who want birds of prey to remain in our skies and who are willing to share some of our habitat, prey animals and facilities with these fine creatures.

This is of vital importance since the future of many species rests, ultimately, with the attitude of private landowners. Most raptors have extensive spatial requirements, occupy special habitats and exist naturally at low densities, such that even our national parks may not be large enough to house viable populations. Natural habitats, and the life they support, are rapidly becoming a rare commodity and people who can maintain such habitats hold a valuable aesthetic, cultural, biological and genetic investment that will appreciate rapidly and make them the envy of the less perspicacious. Graeme and Peter continue, with this book, their talented contribution to helping us integrate our lives with the rich raptor fauna of southern Africa. I join the birds of prey in wishing them every success.

ALAN C. KEMP
Head Curator: Department of Birds, Transvaal Museum, Pretoria

BARRED OWL

7/3/80 Kenton - on - Sea

8.

scale study.

(all primaries barred as shown
on primary 8.)

... and nape paler (umber-tinted) than back.
... ... marks white on head.
... ... back rufous tawn.

left foot
(approx. scale).

Fresh specimen picked up in Donkin Drive
morning of 7/3/80.

Graeme Arnott

INTRODUCTION

This book is about the most magnificent birds that fly – the hunters of the African sky. I freely admit to a certain bias in their favour, but having spent most of my life studying the birds of prey of Africa I can appreciate why poets and Old Testament prophets speak of eagles soaring in the summit of heaven, of Saul and Jonathan being swifter than eagles, or of the way of an eagle in the air. While the larger eagles inevitably attract special attention because of their intrinsic magnificence and power, the birds of prey of Africa as a whole are a fascinating and varied assemblage of species ranging in size from the huge Lappet-faced Vulture to the diminutive Pygmy Falcon.

It is the sheer variety of African birds of prey which makes our continent a cornucopia for "raptorphiles", a word I coined for those who are held in thrall by birds of prey. Although this book is restricted to the 80 species (68 diurnal raptors and 12 owls) occurring in southern Africa, most of them are widely distributed throughout Africa. For the purposes of this book southern Africa is defined as the southern African subregion south of the Cunene, Okavango and Zambezi rivers. However, just as the birds of prey pay no heed to arbitrary man-made boundaries, so also will my text range beyond them as occasion requires.

Birds of Prey of Southern Africa was published in 1982 and is now in its third impression. This is gratifying to myself as author and Graeme Arnott as artist as it indicates that it has fulfilled its purpose as a guide to identification and as a detailed account of the life histories of southern African birds of prey. It serves as a starting point for anyone undertaking research on our raptors, although since 1982 the amount of new information that has accumulated makes a major revision of the text inevitable.

A few examples of species for which our knowledge has been considerably extended are the Bearded Vulture, Black-shouldered Kite and Bateleur, each the subject of an impressive doctoral thesis, while the results of important research projects on the Black Eagle, Pale Chanting Goshawk and African Marsh Harrier have yet to be published. Other species on which significant new information has been published include the Cuckoo Hawk, Forest Buzzard, Red-breasted Sparrowhawk, Osprey, Peregrine Falcon and Scops Owl. Conversely, two of our commonest raptors, the Jackal Buzzard and particularly the Rock Kestrel, still require detailed study of their biology.

Research being undertaken in southern Africa on birds of prey is far in advance of any elsewhere in Africa. The Vulture Study Group has conducted surveys of threatened vulture populations, and in the case of the vulnerable Cape Vulture has produced a comprehensive review of its current status, advance details of which were generously made available to me for the text on page 28. An important part of this group's work concerns the dissemination of favourable vulture publicity and considerable success has been achieved. In the Transvaal a detailed account of the status and conservation of that province's birds of prey has been published and is a model of meticulous research, while in the Cape Province another publication surveys the distribution and status of eagles. Recently the African Raptor Information Centre (ARIC) has been established in the Transvaal and aims to act as a central point for the collection of research information as well as a source of conservation publicity for birds of prey. Linked to ARIC is the publication *Gabar* which deals specifically with African raptors and appositely describes itself as "A Raptor File for Raptorphiles".

The *raison d'être* for *Hunters of the African Sky* is to convey the magnificence and variety of our birds of prey through the artwork of Graeme Arnott in a larger format than was possible in *Birds of Prey of Southern Africa*. The latter's publication in 1982 was the result of close teamwork by author and artist, each indispensable to the other. The collection of information for the text of the book took some fifteen years and a further two years was required to write it all up. For the last six years of this period we collaborated closely on the production of the 24 plates, and an account of this appears later in this book in "The Making of a Picture" (pages 18-25). The considerable reduction of Graeme's original plates to fit the smaller reference book format inevitably meant a loss of quality and, while this did not affect their use for identification purposes, we have both long felt that we would like to see them reproduced in a larger size to bring out the full subtlety of the original colours. Anyone who has seen the book with the large-format reproductions of Norman Lighton's beautiful plates for the early editions of *The Birds of South Africa* by Austin Roberts will appreciate what I mean.

In addition to the original 24 identification plates, Graeme Arnott has painted 10 new scenic plates covering a broad spectrum of our birds of prey. These were chosen somewhat arbitrarily from amongst our favourites, but it so happens that several of them are the focus of current conservation attention. Additionally, in the chapter "The Making of a Picture", a number of "working" paintings have been reproduced. As will be discussed more fully later, these paintings are an important reference source for the artist if his final picture is to impart a feeling of freshness and accuracy.

The text I have written to accompany Graeme Arnott's sensitive and beautiful artwork is of necessity limited by space. However, I have attempted to write something of interest for the general reader who does not profess to have a detailed knowledge of birds of prey. Inevitably some of the material is repetitive of information in *Birds of Prey of Southern Africa*, but wherever possible I have endeavoured to give a different perspective and to introduce new knowledge that has come to hand since 1982 (my sources are indicated in the specific references on page 94.) The text is not intended for raptor experts: my intention has simply been to convey some of the fascination of birds of prey, to draw attention to the threats they face, and to impart some of my wonder at the way they are so well adapted for hunting to survive.

The birds of prey of Africa face many threats, some of which are outlined in the next chapter, and migrants from outside the continent encounter dangers to their survival both in their breeding and in their wintering areas. Southern Africa, as the most developed and industrialised part of the continent, has complex conservation problems by reason of this progress. Despite this, very real advances are being made both in identifying the threats and in seeking solutions. A leading biologist has argued that attempts to save certain species such as the Egyptian, Bearded and Cape Vultures from probable extinction are futile and wasteful as they no longer play a significant rôle in ecological processes since the disappearance of the large migratory herds from the grasslands of Africa. The case for the Egyptian Vulture is arguable because it has already virtually disappeared from southern Africa, and if it were to be reintroduced favourable conditions for its survival would have to be ensured, assuming that this was feasible. The cases of the Bearded Vulture and Cape Vulture are different because their populations are still viable and it has been shown that there is ample food in the form of dead domestic stock; their main threat comes from poisoning and not food shortage. Is their rôle in clearing the veld of carcasses and bones not of ecological and economic importance? Attempts to conserve them surely cannot be construed as either futile or wasteful.

The experiences of my own lifetime have given me cause both for gloom and optimism. I have seen the virtual disappearance of the African Marsh Harrier from the environs of Cape Town, and the steady decline of the southernmost Cape Vulture colony at Potberg in the Bredasdorp district. Conversely, Black Eagle nests on the Cape Peninsula and at Bredasdorp are still active 35 years after I first found them. Both in Zimbabwe and South Africa I have been able to study unmolested breeding birds of prey over many years, and this surely gives one cause for hope when one considers the threatened raptor populations of the northern hemisphere.

In no way do I wish to minimise the many threats to the continued existence of a number of African birds of prey, but one must nourish hope and an awareness in others of their intrinsic merits. If this book serves to engender an admiration for these superb hunters of the African sky then it will have achieved its aim.

BIRDS OF PREY IN A CHANGING WORLD

". . . . . . . but man, proud man,
Drest in a little brief authority,
. . . . like an angry ape,
Plays such fantastic tricks before high heaven
As make the angels weep."
Measure for Measure 11.ii.116

The angels have indeed good cause to weep, not least about the plight of birds of prey. The traditional persecution by those ignorant of their ecological significance undoubtedly still has a deleterious effect, but in recent times it has been the insidious threat of pesticides and loss of habitat that have brought several species to the brink of extinction. An example of habitat destruction within my own experience concerns the Mauritius Kestrel, a species which behaves more like a sparrowhawk and hunts geckos in forested areas. In 1985 I stood with Carl Jones on a mountainside overlooking the Black River forest area, the last remaining fragment on this once thickly wooded island, and saw where new clearings had been made to provide grazing for introduced deer so that sportsmen could hunt them. With infinite patience and dedication Carl Jones had succeeded in breeding this delightful little kestrel in captivity, but if no suitable habitat survives what future is there for it except as a curiosity in captivity? One suggestion that it be released on nearby Réunion is a dangerous one – the kestrel could proliferate there and cause unforeseen problems. Introductions of non-indigenous species should always be avoided: for example, Barn Owls released on the Seychelles to control rats preferred White Terns and have had a serious impact on their numbers; now the Barn Owl has a price on its head there.

There can be no doubt that island birds, whether they be raptors, sea-birds or flightless rails, are the most vulnerable to extinction. The various newsletters of the *World Working Group on Birds of Prey* are a sad inventory of species after species facing threats to their continued existence. Often the dedicated efforts of raptorphiles are negated by greed, ignorance or indifference, particularly where migratory species are concerned. Many Palaearctic birds of prey winter in Africa, but it is their ancestral pattern of movement that places them at risk as they cannot deviate from their instinctive migratory route whatever the threats along the way. In effect this means that for many species protection in their breeding environment is of little value if they are slaughtered on migration.

A few horrendous examples will suffice to illustrate this butchery. It was only some fifty years ago that "sportsmen" assembled on Hawk Mountain in Pennsylvania and literally blasted thousands of migrating birds of prey out of the air. The stench from the rotting corpses was so bad that it led to complaints from farmers below the mountain. Through the efforts of a single dedicated and formidable woman, Rosalie Edge, the Hawk Mountain Sanctuary was proclaimed in 1934 and now some 60 000 people a year visit the sanctuary to enjoy the spectacle. This is a success story. Not so in Malta where, despite legislation to protect birds, they are still shot as they pass through on migration. When conservationists try to protect them they are harassed and assaulted by the hunters – one even had her car blown up – and so the slaughter continues. As recently as 1987 it was estimated that thousands of birds of prey were shot there including hobbies, kestrels and owls, as well as some 50 Ospreys and over 400 European Marsh Harriers. It must be remembered that this represents only part of the northern section of their migratory journey and many are shot before they reach Malta, or at other Mediterranean crossing-points.

In Israel, within two decades, an attitude of indifference or hostility has been turned around into one of intense pride in that country's wildlife. Birds of prey are rigidly protected and under the dynamic leadership of Yossi Leshem of the Israel Raptor Information Centre they are assured of a safe passage through Israel. But once they cross into Lebanon? It is said that the only time that the warring factions cease shooting at each other is when migrating birds pass overhead; then they shoot them out of the sky for food, or just for target practice. One hunter in Lebanon makes his living from taxidermy and specialises in birds of prey. It is estimated that in 45 years he has shot over half a million birds of which 80 000 were raptors. Whether it be via Malta or Lebanon, however, these Palaearctic birds are going to, or returning from, Africa. And when they are there they face the threat of pesticides some of which, unforgivably, are still being shipped to Third World countries even though they have

GRASS OWL
24th June '83

Picked up by Jo Gardner
on Alexandria - Kenton
road near Ghio turnoff.

Kenton - on - Sea.

Graeme Arnott

long since been banned in the industrialised countries that make them. These few examples illustrate that migratory raptors require protection on an international scale to ensure their survival.

Let us now consider the position in southern Africa, particularly South Africa, the most developed part of the continent where industrial and agricultural progress poses more specific problems. The region is intensively farmed and for many large birds of prey their only haven is in the larger national parks. Some species do flourish in man-made environments – the Black-shouldered Kite is a conspicuous and obvious example. Others benefit from certain habitat alterations: stands of alien trees such as eucalypts and poplars, for example, provide breeding and roosting sites for the Black Sparrowhawk which has substantially extended its range in the Transvaal. Conversely, in the Matobo Hills in Zimbabwe, where Black Eagles were intensively studied for twenty years, it has been shown that in designated Communal Land adjacent to the Matobo National Park the eagle population has declined markedly. This is because of the decline of the dassies (hyraxes) which form the staple diet of the eagles. The dassies are unable to compete with goats which graze right up into the hills and denude them of their vegetation cover. In addition the dassies are hunted or trapped by the local people for food and for their skins, which are made into karosses for sale to tourists; a single kaross may contain as many as 36 dassie skins.

Mention of Black Eagles in the Matobos recalls an entirely different threat to our birds of prey – their commercial value. A father and his son, members of a team conducting research on the eagles, were secretly stealing their eggs, and those of other birds of prey, for sale overseas. When the case was brought to court it was found that they had a collection of 800 raptors' eggs, had abused their trust by supplying false information to the research project, and had an incubator for keeping embryos alive prior to smuggling viable eggs overseas for hatching by falconers. The sequel to their case was a raid on a farmhouse in England where eggs valued at £100 000 were discovered. In other cases in southern Africa egg-collectors have been responsible for the systematic robbery of the nests of raptors. Once, in a single season, collectors took eight eggs of rare Lappet-faced Vultures from nests in the Namib Desert.

Falconry also poses a threat, and falcons are much in demand in Arab countries where they fetch very high prices; a Gyrfalcon can be sold for as much as £80 000. Recently, in the U.S.A. and Canada, it was discovered that a number of unscrupulous people, including conservation officials, were smuggling falcons to Arab countries. A three-year undercover "sting" exercise called "Operation Falcon" brought the culprits to book, but the whole sordid business was badly mismanaged and many innocent falconers were unjustly incriminated. Falconry, properly controlled, is a legitimate sport, and falconers impose strict codes of conduct on themselves to prevent this ancient art from falling into disrepute. They are also active in conserving birds of prey and many are leaders in the field when it comes to captive-breeding techniques. In Africa the Zimbabwe Falconers' Club has achieved world-wide respect for the standards it has maintained, and for the success of its captive-breeding programmes. Nothing worthwhile is achieved by driving falconers underground; in my opinion it is far better to legalise their activities and allow them to police their own members within the framework of the law.

Even within the 20 000 square kilometres of the Kruger National Park birds of prey are not necessarily safe, as evidenced by cases of poisoning of vultures in recent years. At one poisoned elephant carcass 121 vultures died, mostly White-backed Vultures, but in other instances species such as the Cape Vulture and Lappet-faced Vulture, classed as "vulnerable" in the Red Data Book, were included among the victims. These poisoning incidents were perpetrated by well-organised gangs of poachers camping inside the Park. The vultures were killed in order to remove their heads, hearts and feet which are used as *muti* (medicine) by herbalists and diviners for their supposed qualities of imparting wisdom, or good luck at the horse-races. Such a threat is a serious one and even if poaching within a national park could be effectively controlled, the large foraging range of the vultures may easily take them into high-risk areas outside the park boundaries on occasion.

Indiscriminate poisoning is probably the most serious threat to scavenging birds of prey in South Africa. Of the 15 raptors listed in the South African Red Data Book on birds, seven are directly affected by poisoning – six vultures and the Bateleur, although the Tawny Eagle probably also merits inclusion in the book. Strychnine is put out for "problem animals" such as jackals but often kills non-target mammals and raptors. One wise conservationist has defined a "problem" animal as one whose use man has yet to discover. Irrespective of whether the animal creates a problem or not, the terrible suffering inflicted before it finally dies from strychnine poisoning can not be condoned on ethical grounds. Despite legislation to control its use, this indiscriminate and inhumane poison appears to be too easily available. A recent survey in the Karoo revealed that it is still widely used and is sold illegally by many pharmacies.

Other forms of poisoning result as a by-product of blanket spraying of queleas, termites or locust swarms, often with banned substances such as Gamma-BHC (Lindane) supplied from Government stocks! The end presumably justifies the means, but no one knows what "end" that might be because these hasty solutions rarely consider the long-term implications, or the many valuable non-target species that may die too. The harrowing story of environmental pollution with chlorinated hydrocarbons which caused a crash in raptor populations in Europe and North America is too well known to discuss here. But long after the dangers were realised and the offending compounds banned, the consequences remained, and still remain. Despite this hard lesson many of these dangerous substances are still being used in Africa. At Lake Kariba in Zimbabwe it has been shown that the eggs of African Fish Eagles are polluted with DDT which is still indiscriminately applied in the catchment areas of the lake. If this situation is glossed over on the grounds that pests must be controlled, or that crops are more important than eagles, let it be noted that these substances do not operate in isolation. It has been established that DDT contamination of human mothers' milk in a sample in Harare was alarmingly high by World Health Organisation standards.

Poisoning is not the only threat faced by vultures in southern Africa and they are among our most threatened birds of prey. Disturbance at their breeding sites and collision with high tension wires, or electrocution on the pylons that support them, are all factors contributing to their decline, particularly in the case of the Cape Vulture. Fortunately the activities of the Vulture Study Group have had a very positive impact on public opinion and there is now a general awareness of the value of vultures. One practical solution has been the establishment of "vulture restaurants"; these supply food as well as the bone fragments so essential for the young in the nest if they are to avoid calcium deficiency and consequent bone deformity. South Africa's Electricity Supply Commission has reacted sympathetically to the electrocution problem by modifying its pylons in areas where vultures are susceptible to electrocution; not only has this measure considerably reduced the vultures' mortality rate but it has also reduced the number of expensive power failures.

This short account of some of the problems faced by birds of prey in a changing, shrinking and often hostile world can only touch on a few of the problems. Our forests are disappearing at a rate too frightening to contemplate, pollutants of every kind reach the remotest places on earth, and the basic cause of much of this – unchecked human population growth – shows no sign of abating. And yet amongst all this gloom for the conservationist there has to be hope, some vision for the future, for without such optimism there can be no solution. Within South Africa there are clear signs that public opinion is turning from either hostility or apathy to one of concern for the environment and its components. The media, especially television, have done much to bring this about, and they can do much more yet. Children in schools must be reached with the conservation message; this applies especially to the underprivileged, who can scarcely be expected to conserve something that could be used to alleviate their immediate hunger. More and more it is being realised that the viability of a conservation area is dependent on the goodwill of the people who live around it.

The sentiments of John Donne apply equally well to a holistic view of conservation: man is not an island but part of an environment where every abuse ultimately threatens him. So when the bell tolls we need not send to know for whom it tolls. It tolls for all of us.

Shows how
warm grey of
wings fades into
white of breast.
These colour tones
are correct.

length of primaries
of closed wing in
relation to tail

Primaries and secs.
pitch black.

SECRETARY BIRD

Picked up by Doug Galpin
in Moneysworth 2/5/85
killed having been
caught on fence.

Graeme Arnott

THE MAKING OF A PICTURE

I met Graeme Arnott when we both lived in Rhodesia (Zimbabwe*) and he was a teacher at the High School in Marandellas (Marondera). At the time I was in the process of gathering material for a book on the identification and life histories of southern African birds of prey and was looking for an artist to paint the plates which were to be an integral part of the project. Graeme's work immediately impressed me with its freshness and accuracy, but without the excessive detail with which so many wildlife artists render their work photographic rather than artistic.

In 1974 Graeme agreed to undertake the onerous task which involved painting twenty-four plates, but at the time neither of us could foresee that it would take six long years to finish them. As we progressed it became clear that schoolmastering and exacting artwork were incompatible – I myself had "retired" from teaching in 1970 to work on the book – so when Graeme suggested that he take up a full-time career as a wildlife artist I backed him in this momentous decision. During the early years things were not easy for him and his family, but the publication of his fine plates in *Birds of Prey of Southern Africa* in 1982 brought him the recognition he deserved. These days his work is much in demand and the lovely artwork in Tony Harris's *Shrikes of Southern Africa* (1988) confirms that he is among the world's leading bird artists.

Graeme left Marandellas and moved to Bulawayo where we were able to work closely on the details of the plates, a task greatly facilitated by the proximity of the Bulawayo Museum which housed the finest collection of bird specimens in Africa, and whose curator, Michael Irwin, gave us enthusiastic assistance in every way and honoured us by contributing his thoughtful Foreword to our book. However, we had not bargained on the Rhodesian bush war, during which all able-bodied men (and many not so able-bodied!) were called up for some form of duty. Graeme and I ended up in the Police Reserve, but because he was younger his commitment was greater than mine and he was more often away from home. This was a serious setback to progress on the plates, especially as other important painting commissions had also to be fitted into a shrinking time schedule. Eventually we both moved to South Africa, Graeme to Kenton-on-Sea in the eastern Cape Province, myself to Cape Town, and the remaining plates were planned through correspondence, phone calls and the occasional meeting. Finally all that remained were the black-and-white drawings to illustrate a number of features not dealt with in the plates but nevertheless requiring illustration. These vignettes did much to enhance the text. When it was all over our relief can not be imagined and the long task may feelingly be described as a "burning chunk" of our respective souls.

No artist develops in isolation – much as some might like to think so – and inevitably there are influences that shape their conception and style. Graeme was fortunate to grow up in an environment which bordered on Wankie (Hwange) National Park where the sights and sounds of bushveld became part of his early perception of the world around him. His innate desire to draw the animals and birds he saw gave expression to his early admiration of these creatures. I can often see in his paintings, where he has no specific scene in mind, the quintessence of these early influences. The mopane woodland scene beneath the Bateleurs soaring magnificently in the frontispiece provides just such an example.

Graeme's work has been influenced by the great British tradition of wildlife artists, and those who have impressed him most are Archibald Thorburn, George Lodge, Charles Tunnicliffe, Eric Ennion, Jack Harrison, George Reid-Henry and his son David Reid-Henry. In more recent times Gordon Beningfield's delightful studies of the English countryside have caught his attention. Nearer home, Heine von Michaëlis' superb work in *Birds of the Gauntlet* (1952) did much to inspire our youthful admiration of birds of prey. No artist, before or since, has matched von Michaëlis' drawings of nestling birds of prey, and he possessed an uncanny ability to look within the soul of his subjects.

David Reid-Henry did as much to inspire Graeme's artistic career as Leslie Brown did for me in my early studies of raptors and this book is dedicated to the memory of our respective mentors. David Reid-Henry was forthright in his views and did not suffer upstart artists gladly – he demolished the widespread admiration of one British so-called bird artist by

---

*For historical accuracy in this chapter original place names have been used with new names in brackets where applicable.

JACKAL BUZZARD ♀ 26/1/82

Barville Park Farm near Port Alfred.
Found drowned in cattle drinking trough
and brought in by Betty Norton.

left foot.

Graeme Arnott

CROWNED EAGLE
immature
Aug '82
(East London Museum).

pointing out that he had drawn a pipit's legs on a kingfisher in a detailed and "accurate" Christmas card study! During his years in Rhodesia he freely assisted Graeme with advice and, while he recognised his talent, he was an exacting and outspoken taskmaster. The genius of his own work was a total inspiration to Graeme who marvelled at his fluid draughtsmanship which produced in his subjects an almost tactile form. There can be no doubt that he had more influence on the early development of Graeme's work than any other man.

David Reid-Henry had himself learnt much from George Lodge, and it is perhaps significant that both were keen falconers. Naturally birds of prey were among their favourite subjects, indeed many artists have been inspired by "the way of an eagle in the air". For many years David was accompanied by an awesome female Crowned Eagle named "Tiara" who brought him a certain distinction and occasional notoriety, as on one occasion when it killed someone's prize Alsatian. David died suddenly in 1977 as we were driving from Bulawayo to Salisbury (Harare) to visit him at his request. He must have sensed that the end was near and perhaps wished to make some arrangements or suggestions regarding his artwork. At best all we could do was to go through all his paintings and sketches with his widow and give as much constructive advice as we could. We were amazed at the number of unfinished pictures, some with only a few minor details to be inserted. But that was typically David – he was such a perfectionist that for want of some reference material such as a plant he would put a picture aside for months, even years, before completing it. It should be noted, however, that he was also easily distracted by the other passions of his life, cricket and falconry. Neither of us will ever forget the feeling of privilege as we looked through the sketchbooks and paintings of one of the greatest wildlife artists of this century.

Flight is one of the most difficult things for a bird artist to depict and most wisely avoid the challenge. Even the great Archibald Thorburn fell down when it came to illustrating gamebirds flying close-up and he was far better when they were in the background of his pictures. Jack Harrison's influence on Graeme's style has also been considerable, not least with flying birds which he drew with an assurance that came from years of close observation and field sketching. He once told me that "sight is a faculty, seeing is an art". Whether this dictum was his own I don't know, but its validity is everywhere apparent in his art. Jack Harrison lived until he was eighty-seven and his final pictures showed no deterioration in their skill or freshness. Such was his assurance in his later years that he could draw a flying bird direct on to his paper without making a tracing or using reference material. We knew him only in the last years of his life, but he was so humble and unassuming about his great talent that he became a much admired friend, despite the considerable differences in our ages. He carried with him at all times a pocket sketchbook in which he would paint miniature water-colour scenes for later reference and it contained some of the most exquisite pictures one could ever hope to see.

Despite other influences on his style, each good artist is, in the final analysis, his own man. In Graeme's work I can see David Reid-Henry's mark in the accuracy of his draughtsmanship, but he places less emphasis on detail, which Reid-Henry somehow combined with such vigour as to prevent it from becoming stifling. Graeme's backgrounds show none of the detail of Reid-Henry and are more reminiscent of Harrison, but the style is entirely his own. One's attention is drawn to the main subject because the background is deliberately muted and yet blends with perfect harmony into the overall composition. Thus habitats are suggested in preference to being treated in minute detail. The Bearded Vulture and Jackal Buzzard are set among cloudy Drakensberg peaks, the Taita Falcon watches over a hazy Zambezi Valley, the Black Harrier quarters over a dry wheatfield, the Pels Fishing Owl hunts above an Okavango backwater, the Barred Owl peers from a thicket in eastern Cape woodland while the African Fish Eagle soars nearby over the Kariega river below Graeme's studio. Only the Cape Vultures have a neutral environment among the clouds, perhaps symbolic of the nebulous nature of their future in the 21st century.

Thus the background to Graeme's artistic approach; now we may consider the techniques used during the preparation of the plates and scenic pictures. The first important ingredient was the accuracy of the draughtsmanship so that each bird looked right. This aspect is what is popularly called "jizz" – a corruption of GISS, an acronym for General Impression of Size and Shape used by the RAF when identifying aircraft. Wherever possible sketches were made of live birds, either in the wild or in captivity, and these were then supplemented by reference for detail to museum skins, sketches of recently dead birds and photographs. For a number of

9 Primary
coverts

4 Alula

18 Sec
cov

Wingspan 6 ft 9 ins.

Graeme Arnott

FISH EAGLE adult ♀ Clock
Picked up dead on 27th August '81

species it was not possible to make drawings from life, in which event it was necessary to rely solely on specimens and photographs. The Bearded Vulture was a case in point: this was one of the earlier plates and at the time Graeme had never seen a Bearded Vulture. When he painted the scenic plate, however, he had thoroughly familiarised himself with this species in the Drakensberg and had made flight sketches.

Having indicated which species were to be included on a plate, I would then suggest the best position to show off the salient field characters of each one. To my mind this latitude is the main reason why artwork is far superior to photographs in a field guide. In many instances the proximity of certain species on a plate would be indicated so as to facilitate comparison between similar ones, for example the Sooty Falcon and Grey Kestrel on Plate 31.

Then it was over to Graeme to work up a design (with each species drawn to scale) which he invariably achieved with the utmost aesthetic appeal, often with a hint of habitat such as grasses or rocks. We had decided at the outset that serried ranks of raptors, all in the same

(greater)

The two innermost secondaries 16 and 17 taper in size and are concealed under longest scapular feathers.

...easurement 580 mm.

... Lloyds Farm, Kariega River. (power line casualty? right wing broken).

frozen posture, was not what we wanted. Not only was the book to be practical, but it also had to have visual appeal. For this same reason the plates themselves were not numbered, and reduced numbered pictures on the facing page were used instead. In most plates the design was such that the birds all looked into the plate and were arranged so that the eye is drawn into and around the plate. Inevitably there was less leeway for composition with the flying plates where, for reasons of economy, many species needed to be included on a single plate. Even here, however, it was possible to vary the style between plates to avoid monotony.

Once we had agreed on a design and the position of each bird, the master tracing was transferred to a tinted neutral background pasted to a firm board. With the wisdom of hindsight we later realised that several of these backgrounds should have been lighter because with reduction some of them became rather murky, a problem that has been avoided by the larger format and different reproduction techniques in this book. Then each species was

MARSH OWL — from life.

16th Oct 81
East London (Carl
Vernon).

sandy.

pale yellow-buff moustache
& eyebrows.

yellowish buff.

lower eyelid shows
paler (grey-neutral)
when sleepy.

iris dark brown.

Toes grey with
greenish tinge.

yellowish sandy buff

RIGHT

painted in detail using No. 3 or 4 Windsor and Newton sable brushes and water-colour paints. Body white or gouache was added where necessary to achieve certain tones, opacity or highlights, and to impart more "punch" than can be achieved with pure water-colour tints and washes. It was also possible to make minor alterations, and these were occasionally necessary, by overpainting with gouache.

The technique for the scenic plates was the same as that for the field guide plates, the background being washed on with larger brushes on to Arches water-colour paper. Sometimes the background would fail for a number of reasons, but at least it could be repeated before the subject matter was painted in detail in the scene. Graeme does not execute water-colour backgrounds *in situ* but relies on his memory, quick pencil sketches of a scene and photographs for his concepts. Photographs are always used as servants, not masters, especially when draughting birds. All too often wildlife "artists" give themselves away by depicting their subjects in awkward or unnatural positions, the obvious result of relying slavishly on a photograph.

Anatomical paintings are an invaluable tool for the artist and they are usually referred to as working or measured drawings, although for practical reasons only smaller species are drawn life-size from measurements. It is time-consuming work and involves detailed drawings of various features of a recently dead bird so that the colours of the soft parts are still fresh. Many leading bird artists have made use of this invaluable source of reference, including Claude Gibney Finch-Davies whose exquisite studies of South African birds are justly famous. Charles Tunnicliffe was probably the greatest exponent of the working drawing and the skill of his draughtsmanship is breathtaking. These "feather-maps" as Tunnicliffe called them are an important source of reference, but they are often works of art in their own right.

Graeme has invested much valuable time in making working drawings over the years, but the effort has been worth it because he refers to them again and again for detail when painting commissions. The Barred Owl is a case in point, and the story of this important specimen is told opposite Plate 9. For two days Graeme worked on a measured life-size drawing and the result is a masterpiece. I covet this picture more than anything that he has painted, but no form of inducement or persuasion will get him to part with it, or with any of his working drawings. They were never intended for sale or publication but are such an integral part of the process of making a picture that we have selected a number of them as examples to illustrate these introductory chapters. In addition to the Barred Owl, the drawings of the Jackal Buzzard and African Fish Eagle were used as reference for the scenic plates, and some of the others during the preparation of the identification plates.

Several years ago Graeme expressed his views on bird art in a letter to me. It was so close to my own thinking that I kept the letter and now quote the most pertinent section:

"I feel that bird art is becoming an endurance test for detail which is only one aspect of a bird's beauty. Equally important is the beauty of line and form animated by the spark of life rather than explored by a short-sighted feather mite. Such aspects are wonderfully realised in the art of Eric Ennion and Jack Harrison."

Perhaps we may leave the last thought to that fine British bird artist, the late Richard Talbot Kelley:

"The artist believes that he can add something to the total appreciation of life by his work. He can remind his fellow men of the perpetual wonder of creation and can, perhaps, point to the daily marvels and lift the corner of the curtain that hides so much of the reason of things."

I BEARDED VULTURE *Gypaetus barbatus*

The Bearded Vulture is to the high mountains what the Bateleur is to the open plains of Africa. As superb fliers each is adapted to its environment, and both impart an aura of majesty to any scene of which they are a part.

The Bearded Vulture resembles a giant falcon except for its long wedge-shaped tail and is perfectly adapted for gliding and manoeuvring in mountainous terrain where it spends 80 per cent of its day in flight.

The taxonomic status of this species is still a matter of contention. The generic name *Gypaetus*, meaning "vulture-eagle", indicates the problem – is it a vulture or an eagle? Certainly it possesses characteristics of both, but it may even be derived from kite stock. Usually it is placed close to the Egyptian Vulture, with which it shares undoubted similarities both in appearance and breeding behaviour.

Whatever its affinities the Bearded Vulture is sufficiently specialised to be placed in its own unique genus. It is a bird of striking appearance and fascinating habits. The rufous colouration of its underparts is an attractive feature, and at one stage there was considerable argument as to whether this was natural pigment or acquired cosmetically. The latter has now been proved by macroscopic analysis to be the case, and the birds derive their rufous colour from contact with iron oxide on ledges or in the cliff caves in which they roost.

The Spanish name for the Bearded Vulture is *El Quebrantahuesos*, "the bone-breaker", and indicates this species' preference for bones. The large 7-centimetre gape enables the bird to swallow large bones up to 18 centimetres in length. Research in southern Africa has established that 70 per cent of its diet consists of bone and marrow which provides 15 per cent more energy than an equivalent amount of red meat. Old bones are preferred and larger ones are picked up and carried lengthwise in the talons to an ossuary, a slab of bare rock on to which the bone is dropped with considerable accuracy from a height of up to 150 metres. If the bone fails to break it may be dropped up to twenty times in succession.

Bearded Vultures nest in sheltered pothole caves during winter. The nest is a large structure of sticks thickly lined with wool and other soft materials. Both sexes share in incubation and brood the chick, a necessary division of duties given the harsh climate during the early stages of the breeding cycle. Usually two eggs are laid but only one chick survives, the second-hatched dying because it cannot compete with its sibling for food. The nestling period is long, about 124 to 128 days, and the young birds may remain with the parents until the following breeding season; even at this stage they are not driven away.

The Bearded Vulture has a wide distribution in the Palaearctic region but has declined drastically in the western part of its range there. In southern Africa it is now confined mainly to the highlands of Lesotho and the Drakensberg escarpment. Elsewhere in Africa it occurs from northern Tanzania northwards to Ethiopia where it is still common. The southern African population has shown a considerable reduction in range which once extended as far as the south-western Cape.

Why has the Bearded Vulture declined in southern Africa? Recent research by Dr Chris Brown shows that poisoning is the major factor causing mortality. A questionnaire survey of the farming community revealed that poisoned baits are still widely used for mammalian predators, but unfortunately are often found by avian scavengers. Dr Brown used radiotelemetry to map the foraging range of a number of Bearded Vultures which he had trapped and found that they had an average home range of 4 000 square kilometres, far too large for them to remain within the boundaries of protected areas. Enlightenment of the farming community is undoubtedly the most important conservation measure. The name Bearded Vulture is now used in preference to Lammergeyer or Lammergeier because these names are too similar to Lammervanger (= "lamb-catcher") and share its unfavourable connotation.

Dr Brown's detailed study estimated the southern African breeding population of the Bearded Vulture at 203 pairs in 1988, 122 of them in Lesotho. If the estimate of young birds is included, then the total population numbers some 630 birds. While this is considerably more than was previously thought, the Bearded Vulture is still a rare species and its population should be regularly monitored.

Graeme Arnott

2 CAPE VULTURE *Gyps coprotheres*

When Van Riebeeck landed at the Cape in 1652 there were Cape Vultures on Table Mountain and they filled the skies of the interior as they followed the vast migratory game herds. As these herds were relentlessly shot out, so the vultures retreated and their colonies declined or ceased to exist. Many a South African mountain or hill bears the name Aasvoëlberg although no vultures fly there now.

The game herds were replaced by domestic livestock, particularly sheep, and the vultures then fed on dead stock. Often the activities of these efficient undertakers of the veld were misinterpreted and they were accused of killing sheep. Carcasses were poisoned in misplaced retribution and this resulted in a high mortality as a single poisoned animal could kill dozens of vultures. Evidence that the vultures had actually killed the farmer's stock was virtually never produced and reports were usually anecdotal. In 1973 the Vulture Study Group was founded and has vigorously promoted favourable vulture publicity in the media, with the result that the attitude of the public towards these maligned birds has changed dramatically. Farmers now rarely poison vultures intentionally, but the latter still suffer from the indiscriminate use of poisons put out for so-called problem animals such as jackals. This poses a threat to all avian scavengers and is something that requires the most urgent attention and solution, especially as present legislation is often ineffective in curbing the misguided and often illegal use of strychnine and other poisons.

The Cape Vulture is endemic to southern Africa and the most recent assessment of the population by researchers of the Vulture Study Group (1985) is 11 938 birds including 4 289 breeding pairs. The main breeding stronghold is the Transvaal with 2 607 pairs, while there are 552 pairs in Lesotho, 530 in Transkei, 255 in Natal, 200 in Botswana and 109 in the Cape Province. The Orange Free State, which once supported a significant breeding population, is down to 31 pairs, while the Waterberg colony in Namibia is now a mere five pairs, down from 500 birds recorded there in 1939.

What factors have caused the decline of this magnificent soaring scavenger? Food supply had always been a variable factor historically and is probably not as serious a problem as poisoning. An important conservation measure has been the establishment of "vulture restaurants" where the birds are fed on a regular basis. This reduces the threat of accidental or deliberate poisoning, and also provides a supply of small bone chips which are specially broken up for the vultures. One cause of nestling mortality was found to be the development of deformities due to a lack of calcium in their diet. Where there are no longer hyaenas to crush up bones, the adults are unable to find suitable chips and bring substitute items such as pieces of china to their chicks.

Electrocution or collision with power-lines has been found to be another serious cause of mortality. The enlightened and concerned attitude of South Africa's Electricity Supply Commission has gone a long way to remedy the problems. The Commission's engineers have concentrated on eliminating the dangers, for example, by providing safe perches for the vultures.

Disturbance at breeding colonies may take the form of direct persecution such as shooting, or trapping by local people to use parts of the vultures for medicines and witchcraft.

Unintentional disturbance is sometimes caused by recreational activities such as mountaineering. Members of the Vulture Study Group volunteer to patrol the areas adjacent to affected colonies over weekends and this has largely solved the problem.

Many Cape Vulture colonies that have disappeared have done so within living memory. My own experience, over three decades, of Africa's southernmost vulture colony at Potberg near Bredasdorp in the Cape is a depressing one. In the 1950s it was still a viable colony: now just a handful of pairs are left. Ironically, recent research has shown that there is more than sufficient food in the form of dead sheep, and one bird fitted with a radio transmitter was found to range no more than 10 to 15 kilometres from the colony. This colony is now part of the enlarged De Hoop Nature Reserve and the vultures are strictly protected and monitored. Only time will tell whether the birds whose soaring abilities I watched with such wonder as a boy will survive into the next century.

Graeme Arnott

3 MARTIAL EAGLE *Polemaetus bellicosus*

The three great eagles of Africa are the Black, Crowned and Martial, each impressive in its own way. The Black Eagle lives in hilly or mountainous country, the Crowned Eagle in forests or well-wooded valleys, while the Martial inhabits a variety of habitats as diverse as the grass-covered foothills of the Drakensberg and the semi-desert scrub of the Karoo.

The Latin and Greek components of the Martial's scientific name stress its ferocious qualities, but it is no more "fierce" than any other bird of prey which survives by killing. However, the large flat head, from which the Afrikaans name *Breëkoparend* derives, imparts a special air of ferocity to this magnificent eagle. Its diet consists of birds, mammals and reptiles, but in common with many other eagles it may occasionally feed on carrion. Gamebirds make up most of its avian diet, but several species of storks have been recorded, and even as large a bird as a Kori Bustard. Leguaans (monitor lizards) are its favourite reptilian prey, but it also kills snakes, even venomous ones such as the Puff-adder or cobras. Mammals caught range in size from small antelope to mongooses. In one remarkable incident in Serengeti, Tanzania, a Banded Mongoose caught by an immature Martial Eagle was rescued by other members of its group. They began to climb the tree in which the eagle was perched three metres above ground and the dominant male reached the eagle, threatened it, and caused it to drop its prey, which then limped off to rejoin its comrades!

The Martial Eagle preys on free-range poultry and is often trapped or shot because of these depredations. Mostly immatures are involved, and of thirty-four specimens in the National Museum in Bulawayo, Zimbabwe, three-quarters were immatures. Domestic small stock losses are often blamed on the Martial, but the only reliable quantitative evidence indicates otherwise. A collection of 346 prey items from nine nests in the Cape Province was analysed and revealed that the eagles were preying mainly on small mammals, as well as birds and leguaans. Only eight per cent of the sample was identified as domestic small stock, most of it from two nest-sites. Some of it may have been taken as carrion, but even if the animals were all killed they were a small part of the total. When considered against the many other threats to domestic small stock the Martial's impact has been grossly exaggerated.

Unlike some eagles, the Martial has no spectacular nuptial display and is not a particularly vocal species. However, its calls are melodious, and some have a close similarity to the fluting *klooee-klooee* . . . call of Wahlberg's Eagle. The nest may be situated in a tree in the neck of a valley where there are air currents, but others may be built in large trees in flat bushveld country. There are recent records from the Karoo of nests on rocky outcrops and on electricity pylons; in one survey thirteen pairs were found breeding on pylons. This has significant conservation implications because the eagles may be expanding into areas which were previously unsuitable due to lack of nest-sites and the population using pylons has been found to be particularly stable.

The normal clutch is a single egg but in one observation two eggs were seen in a nest during an aerial survey. The incubation period is 47-49 days and the male also occasionally incubates. The nestling period is approximately 100 days and the post-nestling period is very variable; some young become independent before the onset of the next breeding season while others may still be present in the nest area. The eagles may breed annually or miss a season like the Crowned Eagle, but some pairs breed on an erratic basis.

The Martial Eagle's inclusion as a Red Data Book species is well justified; it takes at least six years to reach full adult plumage, a single egg is laid, and the birds may breed erratically. In order to maintain the population the adults need to be long-lived and unmolested while breeding. Sadly, outside large national parks, it is declining, and because large territories are required by a pair the eagles are vulnerable when they wander outside the boundaries of smaller reserves. The Martial's future depends to a large extent on the cultivation of new attitudes, when farmers will no longer view eagles as a potential threat but rather express pride at having them on their land.

4 AFRICAN FISH EAGLE *Haliaeetus vocifer*

Few birds have a better claim to be symbolic of the wilds of Africa than the African Fish Eagle. This striking raptor is widely distributed in Africa south of the Sahara and its ringing call is an integral part of the living tapestry of the lakes and waterways of the continent. Voice and appearance both serve the function of territorial advertisement, the former acting as a vocal challenge while the conspicuous white head and breast enable the eagle to proclaim its territory in a passive way while perched. Physical defence of territory may also occur on occasion, and instances of birds found hanging across a branch with interlocked talons may have resulted from aerial battles rather than from cartwheeling courtship flights that carried on for too long. These nuptial flights are impressive, as described by the American poet Walt Whitman for the Bald Eagle, a member of the same genus as the African Fish Eagle. In his *Dalliance of the Eagles* he wrote:

"Skyward in air, a sudden muffled sound, the dalliance of the eagles,
The rushing amorous contact high in space together,
The clinching interlocking claws, a living fierce gyrating wheel. . ."

The African Fish Eagle is adapted for catching fish. In Zululand the average of twelve freshly caught fish was 1,5 kilograms and when the lifting capacity of the eagles was tested experimentally they were found to lift fish up to two kilograms with ease although they struggled to carry fish weighing two to three kilograms. When fish were in the 3-5 kilogram range the eagles could not lift them and had to paddle them to shore using their wings. Surface-swimming fish such as tiger-fish, tilapia, catfish, lung-fish and mullet are the species most frequently caught. Mullet may be snatched from rising waves in the sea, a reminder that in early bird books this eagle was once called the Cape Sea Eagle.

There are records of large numbers of African Fish Eagles gathering at drying pools to feed on trapped catfish. In one exceptional aggregation in Botswana 189 eagles, mostly adults, were counted. Such a large number must have been drawn from an extremely wide area and one wonders just how the "bush telegraph" operates in a case like this. Large numbers of eagles on Lake Malaŵi follow fishing boats for fish offal thrown overboard. In one such incident 61 eagles were counted following a boat rather like seagulls behind a trawler.

Because it is usually thought to be an exclusively fish-eating species, the African Fish Eagle's remarkable versatility is frequently overlooked. It feeds on a variety of types of carrion and is capable of killing birds, mammals and reptiles. As a pirate it probably has few equals amongst African birds of prey. A few examples of its versatility will suffice. It preys on birds up to the size of flamingoes, while at the other end of the scale it may snatch weaver nests to rob them of their contents. It is a dashing predator that has been seen to catch birds such as a Red-knobbed Coot, Cape Turtle Dove and Painted Snipe on the wing. In the Okavango Delta I watched one skim low over a reed-bed at dusk and snatch a roosting weaver with the skill of a falcon. Mammalian prey records include three recently killed dassies (hyraxes). In addition to crocodile hatchlings and leguaans it catches swimming snakes and in one observation it killed one on land. Amphibians are rarely eaten, but like most birds of prey it cannot resist termites.

Piratical attacks on other piscivorous species are regular and it even robs Pied Kingfishers of fingerlings! Other raptors are chased to make them give up their prey and there is a record of a Martial Eagle carrying a large snake being robbed. Perhaps the boldest example of piracy was when an eagle swooped down and snatched a piece of fish from the jaws of a crocodile that was having difficulty swallowing it.

Symbols are not immune to environmental pollution; at one time the American Bald Eagle suffered a serious decline as a result of pesticide residues in rivers and lakes. There is evidence that the African Fish Eagle faces a similar threat, for example on Lake Kariba in Zimbabwe. Contaminated waterways should be carefully monitored because the eagles are merely acting as indicators of a deterioration in the environment that affects us all.

Graeme Arnott

5 JACKAL BUZZARD *Buteo rufofuscus*

This attractive buzzard is endemic to southern Africa where it is widely distributed. It does not occur north of the Limpopo River and is absent from Botswana except for occasional vagrants in the south-east. In the west its range extends as far north as central Namibia, but there is also one record from Damaraland in the north.

The Jackal Buzzard and Augur Buzzard are often considered as a single species, but there are sound reasons for keeping them separate. In southern Africa, except for a grey area of overlap in central Namibia, their distribution is mutually exclusive. In Zimbabwe only the Augur Buzzard occurs and its range extends northwards to East Africa and Ethiopia.

The colourful plumage of the adult Jackal Buzzard makes it easy to identify, but not infrequently individuals have whitish underparts so that they resemble Augur Buzzards. This is undoubtedly the reason for "sightings" of Augur Buzzards well south of their known range. In flight the short red tail and black trailing edge to the wing have led to confusion with the Bateleur, a species which has disappeared from a large part of its former range in southern Africa. Reports of Bateleurs in areas where they no longer occur need to be very carefully authenticated because of probable misidentification by inexperienced observers.

Young Jackal Buzzards are red-brown on the underparts and are quite unlike the adults. In this plumage they are easily confused with other brown "hawks" and identification is no easier in their transitional plumage stages to adulthood. This is but one example of why birds of prey are such a challenging group!

The Jackal Buzzard is normally found in mountainous or hilly country, but in Namibia it may occur in relatively featureless arid terrain. This buzzard is one of the most commonly encountered roadside raptors and in one study area in the Karoo there was an overall density of one bird per 62 kilometres. The study also revealed that although the birds were normally resident some individuals made relatively long-distance movements. One juvenile had moved 640 kilometres in seven months, while two adults moved 332 kilometres and 393 kilometres in three and seven months respectively.

Prey is hunted either from a prominent perch such as a roadside telegraph-pole, or from a soaring position when the bird may hover on slowly winnowing wings. Small mammals such as moles, rats and mice make up a large part of the diet of this species. Birds up to the size of a francolin are caught, as well as lizards and snakes, and termites are also eaten. Items of carrion, including dead sheep, are often eaten, especially in winter. Unfortunately this renders the buzzards liable to poisoning, a fate shared by other scavenging birds of prey.

The buzzards are most vocal at the beginning of the breeding season when they give vent to their loud yelping *kyaah-ka-ka-ka* calls, similar to that of the Black-backed Jackal and the reason for the bird's name. Aerial courtship consists of the male stooping down towards the soaring female with his legs extended.

The nest is normally on a cliff, usually at the base of a bush, but may also be built in a large tree such as a pine. It is a bulky structure of sticks lined with greenery and may be used for several years in succession. The eggs are laid mainly in August and September and the usual clutch is two. Very little is known about the incubation period except that it lasts about 40 days and that the male occasionally incubates. Some females are very aggressive at the nest and will stoop down and strike an intruder.

Cainism is regularly recorded, and the first-hatched chick vigorously attacks its sibling. However, the outcome is not necessarily fatal and there are a number of records of two young being reared together. Hitherto unpublished observations at one nest established that the female stayed with the chick during the first five weeks and fed it on food provided by the male. By this time the chick was able to feed itself and the female then also hunted for prey.

There are no indications at present that the Jackal Buzzard is deliberately persecuted or endangered in any way, but its fondness for carrion places it at risk when carcasses are poisoned. It is a typical roadside raptor and is easily monitored by means of road counts, an ideal method of establishing whether there is any downward trend in its population.

Graeme Arnott

6 RED-BREASTED SPARROWHAWK *Accipiter rufiventris*

The Red-breasted Sparrowhawk is a typical dashing accipiter belonging to a group called "shortwings" by falconers to distinguish them from the falcons or "longwings". It is the African counterpart of the European Sparrowhawk *Accipiter nisus* of the Palaearctic region and the two species are considered to be closely allied. The Red-breasted Sparrowhawk's distribution is rather fragmentary and extends from the western Cape up the eastern half of Africa as far north as Ethiopia.

Although originally dependent on indigenous forest for nesting, it now breeds mainly in plantations of alien species such as pines, poplars and eucalypts. This has enabled it to extend its range, for example into the Karoo in South Africa. However, it is a species that hunts mainly in open country, and it employs several techniques: a spectacular stoop from a soaring position; a fast low dash using cover to surprise its prey; and ambush from a perched position such as in a road through thick cover. Undoubtedly individual birds have an intimate knowledge of their habitat and use surprise, aided by their silent flight, as the main element of attack. Their prey consists almost entirely of birds up to the size of a Red-eyed Dove, a considerable kill that weighs as much as a female Red-breasted Sparrowhawk.

The European Sparrowhawk, the subject of Ian Newton's book *The Sparrowhawk* (1986), is probably one of the most intensively studied raptors in the world. In contrast, the biology of the Red-breasted Sparrowhawk has only recently been studied in any detail. After an impressive 842 hours of observations at nests in the Afromontane environment of Giant's Castle in the Drakensberg, Robert Simmons published three important papers on this species. Subsequently I wrote up observations at two nests in a mosaic of pine plantations and fynbos habitat near Cape Town. The secretiveness of the Red-breasted Sparrowhawk and the fact that its nest is not easily found and difficult to reach, are the main reasons why it had not previously been studied.

These two studies in dissimilar habitats produced strikingly different results, mainly in the size of prey taken. In the Drakensberg study most of the birds caught were small and rarely had a mass exceeding 40 grams, while in the Cape doves were the main prey, usually Laughing Doves averaging 100 grams. Comparisons of prey brought during the incubation, nestling and post-nestling periods showed a far higher biomass in the Cape with, for example, almost seven times as much food being brought in the post-nestling period as was delivered to the Drakensberg nests. It was not so much the quantity as the quality of prey that accounted for the difference between the two studies. It was also found that the nestlings in the Cape left the nest a week earlier than their counterparts in the Drakensberg, and it would seem that the only explanation for this was the better food supply.

The stick nest of the Red-breasted Sparrowhawk is built high in a tree, usually against the trunk. Two to four eggs, usually three, are laid, mainly in late spring (October) in southern Africa. Incubation, almost entirely by the female, lasts for 34 days. The newly hatched chicks are covered in white down and by the time they are two weeks old their first feathers appear on the wings and tail. From then on their feathers develop at a remarkable rate so that by the age of four weeks they are almost completely feathered. The female remains near the nest for most of the nestling period and feeds the chicks on food supplied by the smaller hard-working male. She is remarkably aggressive and will fearlessly attack and strike anyone climbing to the nest. This behaviour is in sharp contrast to that of European Sparrowhawks in Britain where the birds are extremely timid at the nest, the result of bolder birds having been shot out during a long period of persecution by gamekeepers, a process that could perhaps be termed unnatural selection!

The young sparrowhawks leave the nest at a time when there is a plentiful supply of young birds for them to prey on, but initially they develop their skills by chasing each other at high speed through the trees – real kamikaze flying – and by making mock kills of tufts of pine needles or pine cones. These seemingly playful activities serve to equip them for the time when they will make their first kill. Their parents continue to feed them in the nest area until they become independent some five weeks after leaving the nest.

Graeme Arriott

7 BLACK HARRIER *Circus maurus*

The Black Harrier is endemic to southern Africa and has the most restricted distribution of any harrier species in the world. At one time it was thought to be endangered, a misconception that was probably partly due to its nomadic habits. It is an opportunistic species which breeds when conditions are suitable, but in drought years it may not appear in some areas at all, or in reduced numbers. There can be little doubt that increased observer awareness of this species, combined with recent atlassing projects, has resulted in a much better understanding of its true status and distribution.

The Black Harrier is a spring breeder laying mainly in August and September. Its breeding range is almost entirely concentrated in the Cape Province south of 31° S. However, breeding behaviour has been observed in the Orange Free State and has been confirmed in Natal where the eggs were laid in November. There is a post-breeding dispersal from January to July, particularly of young birds, and sightings have been made as far afield as Transvaal, Botswana and Damaraland in north-west Namibia. The main movement appears to be into the more arid regions of the north-western Cape, Kalahari and Namibia, a pattern not unlike that of the Booted Eagle which shares a similar breeding season and range in the Cape Province. No regular pattern is maintained and it appears that the harriers wander opportunistically to areas where there is a good food supply after rain.

Although it inhabits mainly drier country, the Black Harrier may be encountered in a variety of habitats such as montane grassveld, fynbos, renosterbos, agricultural lands and Karoo scrub. Quite often it hunts along road verges because these are the only strips of pristine vegetation in disturbed or overgrazed habitats. It is not dependent on marshy areas for either hunting or breeding as the African Marsh Harrier is, and in the Cape Province where there has been a dramatic reduction of suitable wetland habitat the African Marsh Harrier is far less common than the Black Harrier.

The striking black-and-white plumage pattern, particularly the white rump and broadly banded tail, make this species easy to identify. It is altogether a most handsome bird, even more so at close quarters when the rich yellow cere, eyes and legs can be seen. The sexes are alike, but young birds have a drab brown plumage and a pale abdomen; they are best identified by the characteristic white rump and tail pattern.

Although it may occasionally watch from a low perch, almost all its hunting is done with the buoyant quartering flight so typical of harriers. Sometimes it stoops several times in one spot to try to flush out prey, or it may hover on slowly winnowing wings low over the ground if it sees something. In common with most owls, its flight is silent, and this enables it to listen for prey as it flies slowly along. The Black Harrier may hunt in poor light well before sunrise and late into the evening when it is almost dark. Its prey consists of birds, rodents, amphibians, insects and the occasional lizard, but it has been recorded eating a dove's eggs and may also eat carrion.

The breeding habitat of the Black Harrier is very varied. Nests have been found in mountain fynbos amongst ferns, in low scrub in sandveld, in renosterbos on an arid hillside, in agricultural lands and in long grass or low reeds in marshy areas. The amount of nest material varies according to site; sometimes just a small pad of grasses on the ground will suffice, while at other times in marshy ground a platform of sticks is built and lined with grass.

Clutches of two to five eggs are laid and they hatch after 34 days. Only the female has been recorded as incubating and she rarely leaves the nest except to receive food from the male in an aerial food-pass typical of harriers. The young spend about five weeks in the nest, closely attended by the female in the first two weeks. Throughout the nestling period the male is the main food provider, usually passing food to the female in flight, but occasionally he may land briefly at the nest to drop prey.

An interesting feature of the Black Harrier's breeding biology is the proximity of nests at times, in one case two nests were only 50 metres apart. Polygyny has been suspected but not proved, and it is an aspect of their breeding behaviour that merits further investigation.

8 TAITA FALCON *Falco fasciinucha*

This exquisite little falcon has the proportions of a small Peregrine and is every bit as impressive in pursuit of prey. First collected in 1895 at the Taita Hills in south-eastern Kenya, it has apparently not been recorded there in recent times. Its distribution is confined to the eastern part of Africa from Zimbabwe to southern Ethiopia, but it is nowhere common, indeed it is probably one of the rarest falcons in the world.

The specific name *fasciinucha* means "banded nape" and draws attention to its most important field characteristic, the rufous patches at the back of the head. The only other species with which it is likely to be confused is the African Hobby from which it may be distinguished by these nape patches and its whitish throat. In flight it has the stocky proportions of a Peregrine rather than the slender, almost swift-like, silhouette of the African Hobby.

This falcon occurs in mountainous country, or sheer gorges, in areas of relatively low rainfall. At the first Pan-African Ornithological Congress at the Victoria Falls in 1957 two visiting ornithologists, Leslie Brown and Dick Herbert, recorded the Taita Falcon there for the first time, although it had been recorded elsewhere in Zimbabwe, and a procession of distinguished ornithologists went to view the falcons in the gorge below the Victoria Falls Hotel. Until recently the only worthwhile observations have been made at the Victoria Falls, but the pairs that nest there have unfortunately also attracted the unwelcome attentions of egg-collectors. Nevertheless it would seem that the precipitous gorges of the Zambezi Valley provide a stronghold for them and they are probably not presently endangered. Their rarity, however, leaves no room for complacency.

The Taita Falcon spends long periods perched on a cliff, or on the branch of a tree growing out from it, and it can easily be overlooked during these periods of inactivity. It flies with characteristic rapid, shallow wing-beats and gains height quickly. At the Victoria Falls I have watched the resident swifts pre-empt a surprise attack by circling above the falcon and staying above it as it ascends. In attack it makes a spectacular stoop on a bird, either striking it directly, or diving past and swooping up to take it from below. It preys mainly on small birds such as bulbuls, queleas and weavers, but larger species such as Green Pigeon, Purple-crested Lourie, Red-winged Starling and a young Helmeted Guineafowl have been recorded. The young guineafowl was part of a flock flying across a gorge and the falcon was watched feeding on its quarry for two hours.

The only quantitative prey study (240 items) was at a nest on Mount Elgon in Uganda on the Kenya border where an intrepid German ornithologist made detailed observations from a hide suspended over a sheer cliff. He established that during the first half of his study the prey consisted mainly of swifts, swallows and martins, but when these species moved away on migration the falcons switched their attentions to weavers which were common in nearby cultivated lands.

The nest-site is a hole in a sheer cliff and those in the Victoria Falls gorges are typically in small erosion holes in the basalt cliffs. Three to four eggs are laid in a shallow scrape at the back of the hole. The male assists with incubation and at the Mount Elgon nest he sat three or four times a day for up to 140 minutes with an average of 37 minutes during sixty spells on the nest. An incubation period of 26 days was obtained at the Victoria Falls while at Mount Elgon it was 31 days. The male assists the female in brooding the chicks initially, but his main task is to keep her supplied with prey for the young. The nestling period is approximately six weeks and the young falcons continue to be fed for several weeks after leaving the nest.

Why is the Taita Falcon so rare? Competition for food with the larger Peregrine and Lanner would not seem to be the reason. In an area surveyed on Mount Elgon, where all three species occurred, the observer located 19 pairs of Peregrines, five pairs of Lanners and four pairs of Taita Falcons. It appeared that all suitable nest-sites were taken up and were fiercely defended by the resident pairs. The Taita Falcon, as the smallest of the three, would presumably suffer in competition for nest-sites. However, as with the inexplicably rare Ayres' Eagle, the reasons for the Taita Falcon's rarity still require further elucidation.

Graeme Arnott

9 BARRED OWL *Glaucidium capense*

The Barred Owl here illustrated is the subject of a fascinating story, but in order to understand its significance we must first briefly examine the history of this species. The bird shown here belongs to the nominate race *Glaucidium capense capense* which was first described by Dr Andrew Smith in 1834 on the basis of two specimens from the eastern Cape Province. This notable naturalist, a medical doctor, made a number of important collecting expeditions and his interest in reptiles earned him the distinction of being the father of herpetology in South Africa. He was appointed the first Director of the South African Museum in Cape Town in 1825 and later in his career was knighted for his work as Inspector-General of Army Hospitals during the Crimean War.

Having been collected and described, the Barred Owl then "disappeared" from the eastern Cape for some 150 years. The four subsequent records of the nominate race were all from Natal and Zululand and it was generally thought to be extinct in the eastern Cape. Then, on 7 March 1980, a freshly dead Barred Owl was picked up early one morning in Kenton-on-Sea and taken to Graeme Arnott who spent two days executing meticulous working drawings of this exciting find (see pages 8 and 9). The owl was then deep-frozen and forwarded to Dr P. A. Clancey, Director of the Durban Natural History Museum, who was delighted at its rediscovery as he had never accepted the view that it no longer occurred in the eastern Cape.

Subsequently a Barred Owl was seen and photographed in the Hluleka Nature Reserve in Transkei in 1981, and further birds have been called up in the eastern Cape using tape recordings. In addition to the dead specimen, Graeme Arnott has since sketched the bird in the wild and these field drawings form the basis for this painting and its setting. The "disappearance" of the Barred Owl in the eastern Cape illustrates the elusiveness of owls, and indeed as recently as 1965 a species new to science, the Sokoke Scops Owl, was discovered in the Sokoke Forest in coastal Kenya.

Despite the elusiveness of the eastern Cape Barred Owls, this species is widely distributed and not uncommon in suitable woodland in the north of its range where it occurs alongside another member of its genus the Pearl-spotted Owl. The two species are superficially similar in appearance, but the Barred Owl is larger and dumpier with more of a "puffball" head in contrast to the almost elfin appearance of the Pearl-spotted Owl. As their respective names suggest, the main difference in appearance is the barring of the dorsal plumage of the one in contrast to the spotted pattern of the other.

The voice of the Barred Owl is a mellow repetitive *krrooo, krrooo, krrooo . . .* not unlike the call of a Cape Turtle Dove. It has none of the vivacity and volume of the piercing crescendo whistle of the Pearl-spotted Owl, one of the most characteristic sounds of the African bush, but it is nevertheless easily recognised when heard. It often calls and moves about during daylight when it may catch prey, in one case a 30-centimetre-long snake. The talons are large for its size, but the limited observations of its diet suggest that it feeds mostly on insects. Other recorded items include lizards, mice, a bird and a frog. Like the Pearl-spotted Owl, it is probably capable of capturing quite large prey at times, but further prey records are needed to establish a better picture of what it eats.

The breeding biology of the Barred Owl is not well known. It nests in natural holes in trees and has not yet been found to use woodpecker or barbet nest-holes, probably because it is too large to enter them. It has been observed to carry green leaves into the nest, a rare instance of any owl using nest material. Interestingly, similar behaviour has been observed in the Pearl-spotted Owl. Usually three white eggs are laid and the incubating bird sits very "tight" if the nest is inspected. The incubation period is unknown and the nestling period is approximately five weeks. Anyone who could study a single breeding cycle would add significantly to our meagre knowledge of the breeding biology of this attractive species.

Graeme Arnott

IO PEL'S FISHING OWL *Scotopelia peli*

This large and beautiful owl is the commonest of three species of African fishing owls and is widely distributed in lowland areas of tropical Africa. The Vermiculated Fishing Owl is confined to the Congo Basin while the Rufous Fishing Owl is known on the basis of a few specimens from the rain-forests of West Africa. The biology of these two species is virtually unknown, but Pel's Fishing Owl has been quite well studied.

This owl is named after a Dutch government official H.S. Pel who worked on the Gold Coast (now Ghana) between 1840 and 1850. The species was first described in 1850 and the first illustration appeared in 1859 in volume one of *Ibis*, the prestigious journal of the British Ornithologists' Union. The colour picture was executed by the renowned bird artist Joseph Wolf at the request of J.H. Gurney, an early authority on birds of prey, who had been presented with a live specimen from West Africa.

The African fishing owls, like Asian fishing owls of the genus *Ketupa*, are characterised by their unfeathered legs and feet, as well as by long, sharp claws and spiny projections on the soles of their feet. These are adaptations for fishing similar to those of the Osprey and African Fish Eagle. Most owls fly silently, but this is not the case with the fishing owls as they have no need for a muffled approach to their underwater quarry.

The most detailed observations on Pel's Fishing Owl, mainly by a single observer, have been made in the Okavango Delta in Botswana. Here they were found to eat mainly fish, although the diet also includes occasional frogs, crabs and freshwater mussels. Fish caught usually weighed between 100 and 250 grams and the heaviest was two kilograms. Although a variety of species was recorded, catfish, squeakers and the African Pike were most frequently taken. Interestingly, quite often just the head of the fish was eaten and the body discarded.

Pel's Fishing Owls inhabit areas with large trees near water. During the day they conceal themselves amongst the thick foliage and are extremely difficult to locate unless they are disturbed and take to flight. Usually they settle in another leafy tree some distance away and, unless the spot has been carefully noted, they are not easy to find again. Often the birdwatcher is treated to a series of frustrating glimpses, but occasionally they will settle in a more open spot where they can be fully appreciated as they stare at the observer with their large dark eyes.

This species is strictly nocturnal and emerges at dusk to hunt where there are still pools or quiet backwaters. A favourite hunting perch is a low branch over water, as illustrated here, but they may also fish from sand-banks. They locate fish by movement on the surface of the water and swoop down, throwing their long legs well forward at the moment of impact, at the same time drawing the nictitating membranes across the eyes to protect them from damage.

The call of the Pel's Fishing Owl has often been fancifully described as a weird wailing, "like a lost soul falling into a bottomless pit", but this eerie sound is in fact produced by the young owl when it begs for food, or by the female when the male brings food for her at the nest. The usual call is a series of deep sonorous hoots, *hoommmmmmmm-hut*, often produced in conjunction with low grunts. On a still night it carries across the sounding board of water for up to three kilometres. The female also makes a strange high-pitched trilling and screaming call during a distraction display near the nest. She walks up and down a branch with spread wings and then drops into the undergrowth where she flops about until approached too closely and then she flies off normally.

The breeding season is timed so that eggs are laid when the water level is highest; by the time the chicks hatch the level has dropped and prey is more easily captured. Normally two eggs are laid in the fork of a large tree or in a natural hollow, but only one chick is reared, the second one presumably dying of starvation. The young owl leaves the nest while it is still mainly downy and only acquires adult coloration when it is about a year old. It remains with its parents for many months and is particularly slow at learning to catch fish for itself.

In South Africa Pel's Fishing Owl is an uncommon species found mainly along the large river systems of Zululand and the northern Kruger National Park. The main threats to its survival would be the destruction of riparian forest and the silting up of rivers. Fortunately it is still widespread and relatively common in the Okavango Delta, one of the best areas to see this species.

Graeme Arnott

II BLACK EAGLE *Aquila verreauxii*

This magnificent eagle is considered by many to be the finest in Africa and it imparts a grandeur to any mountain setting as it soars overhead with consummate grace. The characteristic leaf-shaped wings are adapted for soaring in mountainous country and it is impressive to watch how rapidly the eagle can gain height on rising air currents or manoeuvre close to a cliff.

The Black Eagle has been aptly described as the ecological equivalent of the Golden Eagle of the northern hemisphere and the two species undoubtedly share many similarities. Fortunately, the Black Eagle has not been subjected to widespread persecution like the Golden Eagle and is not presently under serious threat anywhere in Africa.

The name Black Eagle is used exclusively in southern Africa, but elsewhere it is usually called Verreaux's Eagle, a name that derives from a Frenchman Jules Verreaux, one of three brothers who visited southern Africa in the first half of last century to collect specimens. Even if the name Black Eagle becomes generally accepted, Jules Verreaux will remain commemorated in the scientific name of the species.

The Black Eagle has the distinction of being the most intensively studied eagle in Africa and probably in the world. This is because Valerie Gargett, a dedicated amateur ornithologist in Zimbabwe, studied a concentrated population in the Matobo Hills south of Bulawayo. She headed a survey team of enthusiastic week-end birdwatchers which monitored the biology of the eagles, particularly their breeding success, over a period of twenty years. The hills are an optimum environment because the numerous rocky outcrops provide nesting-sites for the eagles and ideal habitat for the dassies (hyraxes) which make up the bulk of their prey. Her research established that the eagles in the protected Matobo National Park area bred successfully while those in adjacent communal land were adversely affected because the local inhabitants trapped the dassies for food and to make karosses for the tourist trade, while their cattle and goats depleted the available food supply of the dassies.

There has been no long-term study of Black Eagle biology that is comparable to the research undertaken in the Matobos. In the Cape Province and Transvaal the populations of these eagles have been assessed, but nowhere has a density been found to match that of the Matobos where it is approximately one pair per 10,5 square kilometres. Recently a Ph.D. student has studied Black Eagles in the Karoo National Park and the published results will prove extremely interesting. One technique he has used is time-lapse photography with small cine cameras which are able to monitor activity at the nest. Cameras can be placed at different nests and the only limiting factor is the life of the batteries which have to be changed periodically. In one remarkable instance the camera revealed that a downy eaglet was killed and eaten by a mongoose, a disappearance that would otherwise have been noted as "cause unknown".

Black Eagles are extremely prey specific and in the Matobos dassies made up 98 per cent of 1 892 prey items recorded. This predilection for dassies is found throughout their range. They also prey on other mammals such as small antelopes, occasional goat kids and lambs, squirrels and mongooses. In common with many eagles they also feed on carrion, so that the remains of a lamb on a nest is not necessarily evidence that the eagles killed it. Unfortunately the eagles may come down to a poisoned carcass or be caught in a gin-trap set for a caracal, but any farmer who deliberately destroys Black Eagles on his land is undoubtedly unaware of the implications. Dassies compete with sheep for grazing and if the eagles are locally exterminated they lose their fear and forage well out into the open veld away from the hills. They also prey on birds, particularly guineafowl, and they have been seen to take Cape Vulture chicks. Reptilian prey includes lizards, snakes and tortoises; in two separate observations tortoises were carried to a height and dropped to break them open.

Breeding biology has been intensively studied, even to the extent of counting the 1 569 pecks during 72 hours that a first-hatched eaglet inflicted on its sibling before killing it. Recently Black Eagles have been found nesting on an electricity transmission pylon and on a microwave tower, the first records of this species using man-made structures. Thus, even in the case of an intensively studied species such as the Black Eagle, there is always more to be found out.

12 BATELEUR AND SECRETARY BIRD

The two species depicted here could not have more contrasting hunting techniques. The Secretary Bird, aptly described as a "long-legged marching eagle", covers large areas with its 40-centimetre stride, while the specialised aerodynamics of the Bateleur enable it to forage at a low altitude to search for carrion or drop opportunistically on to unsuspecting quarry.

The Secretary Bird is said to have acquired its name because of a similarity to a clerk with a quill pen placed behind his ear. A more plausible explanation is that the name derives from the Arabic *saqr et-tair*, which may be loosely translated as "hunter-bird", a name subsequently corrupted into French as *secrétaire*. Although the Secretary Bird may not be a raptor at all and might have evolved from crane-like ancestors, it certainly has all the attributes of a bird of prey and is placed in its own unique family, the Sagittariidae.

The diet of the Secretary Bird includes almost anything it can overpower. In one analysis of prey in the Kruger National Park 87 per cent of 1 124 items was comprised of grasshoppers with snakes making up less than one per cent. Sentiment towards this species is favourable because it is thought to kill many snakes, a typical example of a warped value judgement because snakes are themselves beneficial. The Secretary Bird is still widespread and relatively common in South Africa; in some regions it has benefited from bush clearance which has created new habitats. Conversely, urban sprawl and monoculture farming has driven it out of other areas. Whether the indiscriminate spraying of poisons during locust outbreaks has adversely affected local populations is not yet known.

The Bateleur is one of the most impressive hunters of the African sky. Its characteristic flight silhouette, colourful appearance and fast cross-country gliding technique all draw our attention to it. Sadly, the very attributes that make it such an efficient low-level forager are also responsible for its dramatic drop in numbers in recent years. The Ph.D. thesis of Richard Watson, who studied the Bateleur in the Kruger National Park for four years, revealed that it is remarkably efficient at locating carrion, even very small items which were put out to test its abilities experimentally.

The Bateleur has disappeared, often within living memory, from many areas where it previously occurred, for example from 70 to 80 per cent of its former range in the Transvaal. It is now a Red Data Book species in South Africa with its main population of 400 to 500 pairs in the Kruger National Park. Elsewhere in South Africa it is largely confined to national parks while in Zimbabwe and Zambia it is also declining.

The most important cause of the Bateleur's demise is poisoning because it easily locates baits put out for "problem" mammals by stock-farmers. While direct persecution has also played a part, as has habitat destruction, the Bateleur will not grace the skies of its former range until the unselective and irresponsible practice of relying on poisons for controlling mammalian predators is brought to an end.

1 Bateleur: adult female
2 Bateleur: juvenile
3 Bateleur: adult male with creamy-coloured back
4 Bateleur: adult male
5 Secretary Bird: adult
6 Secretary Bird: juvenile

13 BEARDED VULTURE AND SMALL VULTURES

The four species shown here share superficial similarities and have long been the subjects of taxonomic contention. Perhaps closest are the Bearded and Egyptian Vultures, but they are best kept in separate genera. The Palm-nut Vulture, also known as the Vulturine Fish Eagle, has variously been linked with fish eagles, the Egyptian Vulture and, more recently, with the snake eagles. The Hooded Vulture appears very similar to the Egyptian Vulture because of its bill shape, but this is an example of convergent evolution and they are not closely related. All four species are either rare or threatened in some way in southern Africa (see p. 26 for comments on the Bearded Vulture) and all are included in the South African Red Data Book on birds.

The Palm-nut Vulture is widely distributed in Africa south of the Sahara and is locally common, for example in Angola and The Gambia. The species is closely linked to the distribution of oil palms and feeds on their fruits. In South Africa the known breeding population of three pairs is confined to Zululand where they are dependent on groves of *Raphia* palms. Immatures appear to wander widely and have been recorded in a variety of scattered localities in southern Africa. A number of these sightings, especially in the north, almost certainly involve wandering Angolan birds. The Palm-nut Vulture is very much a peripheral species in southern Africa and as a breeding species it is confined to areas of *Raphia* palms in Zululand.

The Egyptian Vulture was formerly widespread in southern Africa but probably never in large numbers. It is now extremely rare with fewer than 30 sightings since 1945. It may possibly still breed in remote areas of the Transkei but there is no recent evidence. Its decline has been linked to a combination of factors: the disappearance of the migratory game herds; poisoning; the general improvement in sanitation; and direct persecution, particularly by ostrich-farmers because of its remarkable habit of breaking open ostrich eggs by throwing stones on to them. Elsewhere in Africa, and throughout its Palaearctic range, it is locally common, particularly where relatively primitive human conditions prevail. There is no evidence that the migratory population of the Palaearctic reaches southern Africa.

The Hooded Vulture may be termed the "tail-end Charlie" amongst the vultures and it cannot compete with the larger species at a carcass. Its speciality is to glean scraps once the other vultures have fed and its long thin bill is ideally suited for this. In South Africa it is rare with almost the entire breeding population of some 50 pairs confined to the Kruger National Park. Elsewhere in sub-Saharan Africa it is widely distributed and locally very common, especially where meat is handled in outdoor abattoirs and market places as in West Africa. It thrives where sanitary conditions are primitive and in addition to offal it eats both human and animal faeces. Under such conditions its value is recognised and it is not persecuted.

1 Palm-nut Vulture: adult
2 Palm-nut Vulture: juvenile
3 Hooded Vulture: adult
4 Hooded Vulture: juvenile
5 Bearded Vulture: immature
6 Bearded Vulture: adult
7 Egyptian Vulture: adult
8 Egyptian Vulture: juvenile

G.G.Arnott

14 LARGE VULTURES

The Cape Vulture, endemic to southern Africa, is classed as a "vulnerable" species by conservationists (see p. 28) while the closely related White-backed Vulture is the commonest and most widespread vulture in Africa. However, the latter is not spared from the threat of poisoning, even in a protected area like the Kruger National Park, where substantial numbers were recently poisoned by poachers, who required their body parts for magico-medical purposes.

The two species differ markedly in their nesting requirements, the Cape Vulture breeding colonially on steep cliffs, while the White-backed Vulture nests in loose groups in tall trees, usually along a watercourse. At carcasses the Cape Vulture is dominant, as may be expected because it is larger and heavier. Nevertheless the two species compete for the easily accessible meat and entrails while the Lappet-faced Vulture, able to dominate all other vultures at a carcass at will, often chooses to stand aloof at first, only moving in later to rip off pieces of hide and ligaments with its powerful bill.

The White-headed Vulture, the most handsome of all African vultures, is often one of the first scavengers to arrive at a carcass and probably follows Bateleurs. It is unable to compete with other vultures once they come down in force, so needs to feed quickly if it is to get anything at all. It is largely solitary in its habits and appears to subsist mainly on smaller carcasses it finds. There are a few direct observations, and much circumstantial evidence, which indicate that it may regularly kill for itself. Like the Lappet-faced Vulture it has strong toes and curved claws, which supports the view that both species can make their own kills. The White-headed Vulture is also a pirate and robs other scavenging birds of food.

The range of the Lappet-faced Vulture in South Africa has declined markedly; it has disappeared from most of the Cape Province and in the Transvaal there are probably fewer than 40 breeding pairs. The Transvaal vultures may depend on neighbouring countries such as Botswana and Zimbabwe for maintaining a viable breeding population and in the Transvaal the Lappet-faced Vulture is considered the most threatened vulture species. It is uncertain to what extent, if at all, the range of the White-headed Vulture has decreased, but it is now confined to proclaimed conservation areas in South Africa. Both species are vulnerable to the ever-present threat of poisoning and direct persecution such as shooting must inevitably have played a part in their decline. The Lappet-faced Vulture is a species particularly sensitive to disturbance at the nest.

The Lappet-faced Vulture is often found in arid areas and in Namibia occurs throughout the Namib Desert. Recent research has shown that predator-control poisoning operations are the most serious threat to this species there. One can only hope that public-awareness campaigns aimed at farmers will be effective so that Namibian birds do not suffer the fate of the Lappet-faced Vultures of the Negev Desert in Israel where the species is on the brink of extinction.

1 White-backed Vulture: adult
2 White-backed Vulture: juvenile
3 White-headed Vulture: juvenile
4 White-headed Vulture: adult female
5 Lappet-faced Vulture: juvenile
6 Lappet-faced Vulture: adult
7 Cape Vulture: juvenile
8 Cape Vulture: adult

G G Arnott

15 SECRETARY BIRD AND VULTURES

The largely terrestrial habits of the Secretary Bird conceal the fact that it is an accomplished soarer, sometimes rising to a great height on thermals; in one observation a pilot recorded a bird at 3 800 metres above ground level. Undulating nuptial displays, similar to those of other birds of prey, are performed during soaring flights. During the breeding season, when the birds forage far afield to find food for their nestlings, they will often fly up on a thermal on the return trip and then drop from a considerable height to land near the nest. This strategy saves a long walk back and thus conserves energy. Immature Secretary Birds may be identified in flight by their brownish underwing coverts with a white bar across them.

The White-headed Vulture shown here is a female and illustrates how even an obvious case of sexual dimorphism can be overlooked. It was only when the plate was completed that evidence was published which established that males have grey, not white, secondaries. The difference in the colour of the secondaries also shows on perched birds, so it is strange that this characteristic was not noticed until recently.

Adult Cape and White-backed Vultures in flight are frequently mistaken for one another and the distinctions are subtle. The Cape Vulture is generally whiter in appearance with paler secondaries and usually there is a row of black spots along the junction of the underwing coverts and the flight feathers. In view of the decline of the Cape Vulture, and the importance of sightings from peripheral areas of distribution, care is needed before submitting a record. The immatures of the Lappet-faced and White-headed Vulture could be confused with each other and with both the adult and the immature Hooded Vulture, an example of one of the many difficult areas in the identification of raptors. While it is easy to write that size differences are considerable, this doesn't help when the birds are soaring high overhead. Their identification is something that can only be learnt from experience and careful reference to a plate such as the one opposite.

The distinctive flight outline of the Bearded Vulture distinguishes it from all other raptors, except that the immature could possibly be confused with an immature Egyptian Vulture which has a similar tail shape. The Egyptian Vulture is now extremely rare in southern Africa and the greatest circumspection is needed, and preferably a photograph, before a sighting can be confirmed. The adult could be confused with the Palm-nut Vulture, but the distinctive differences in silhouette and the underwing pattern are diagnostic. Other raptors which are superficially similar to the Egyptian Vulture are pale Tawny Eagles and the pale plumage form of the Booted Eagle, but both these lack the characteristic diamond-shaped tail of the Egyptian Vulture.

The care required in identifying the Egyptian Vulture underlines an important principle of raptor identification; before deciding that something is a rarity, and thus obviously more exciting for the observer, always eliminate the unlikely first and only work back to the rarity once all the more likely options have been considered.

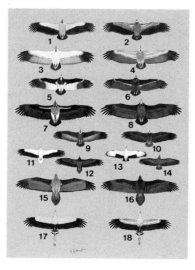

1   White-backed Vulture: adult
2   White-backed Vulture: juvenile
3   Cape Vulture: adult
4   Cape Vulture: juvenile
5   White-headed Vulture: adult female
6   White-headed Vulture: juvenile
7   Lappet-faced Vulture: adult
8   Lappet-faced Vulture: juvenile
9   Hooded Vulture: adult
10 Hooded Vulture: juvenile
11 Egyptian Vulture: adult
12 Egyptian Vulture: juvenile
13 Palm-nut Vulture: adult
14 Palm-nut Vulture: juvenile
15 Bearded Vulture: adult
16 Bearded Vulture: juvenile
17 Secretary Bird: adult
18 Secretary Bird: juvenile

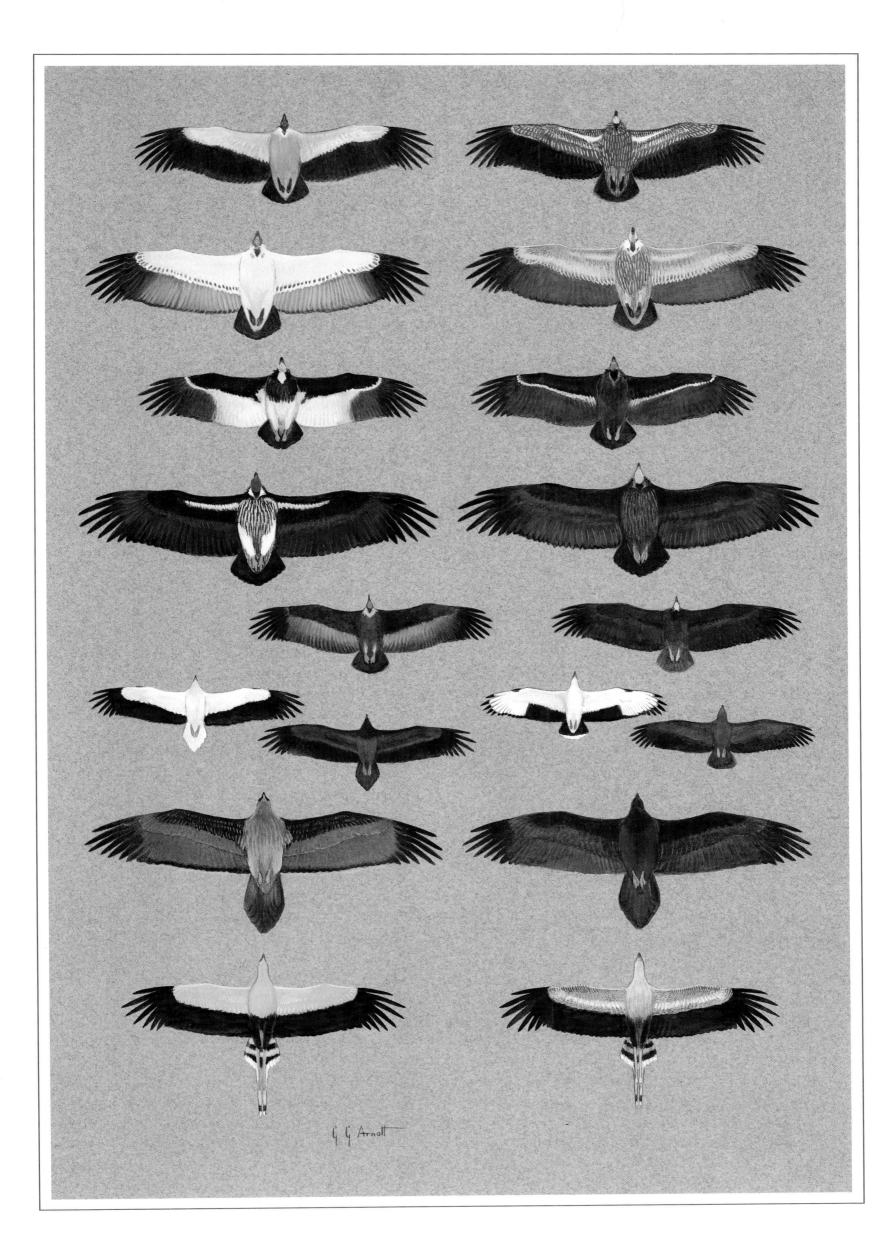

G. G. Arnott

16 KITES, CUCKOO HAWK, BAT HAWK AND HONEY BUZZARD

The species depicted here include some of the most fascinating of Africa's birds of prey. The ubiquitous Black-shouldered Kite is probably one of the commonest raptors in southern Africa and has been intensively studied. The energetics of its hunting techniques have been calculated and, for example, although it uses seven times more energy while hovering, this results in twice the number of kills made when hunting from a perch. Its diet consists almost entirely of rodents – 98 per cent in one large sample from the Transvaal. An interesting aspect of the timing of the breeding season is that it could be linked directly to the gonadal activity of its prey – the reproductive steroids of the rodents may give the kites advance warning of an impending breeding cycle and thus trigger their own hormonal activity. Ringing and colour-marking have established that Black-shouldered Kites are highly nomadic. Although birds may appear to remain in an area, there is in fact a continual turnover in the population.

The Black and Yellow-billed Kites belong to a group collectively known as the *Milvus* kites, and they are in a different genus from the Black-shouldered Kite. The Black Kite is a summer visitor from the Palaearctic while the Yellow-billed Kite is an intra-African migrant. The *Milvus* kites are widely distributed in the Old World and are some of the most successful of all raptors. This is undoubtedly due to their versatility, and, in addition to being dashing hunters, they are also accomplished pirates and scavengers.

The Cuckoo Hawk, previously inappropriately known as the Cuckoo Falcon, is an unobtrusive species. It hunts from a perch and drops on to its prey which consists mainly of insects, particularly grasshoppers, but also lizards, small snakes, chamaeleons and occasionally small birds and rodents. The Cuckoo Hawk's breeding biology is fairly well known, mainly as the result of recent studies. An interesting peculiarity is the number of small leafy branches used in the construction of the nest; these are snipped off using its notched bill-tip which acts like a pair of secateurs.

Another insect-eating specialist, the Honey Buzzard, is somewhat of an enigma in Africa. Although large numbers cross into Africa from the Palaearctic, they are nowhere common and in southern Africa they are rare. Despite its name, the Honey Buzzard is more adapted for eating the larvae and pupae of wasps, as its Afrikaans name "Wespevalk" (wasp hawk) correctly indicates.

The crepuscular Bat Hawk is another specialist with fascinating habits. It roosts in trees during the day and makes no particular effort to conceal itself. It has white spots on its nape and white eyelids, so the sleeping bird appears to be looking both ways, like the Roman god Janus, an adaptation that presumably deters potential predators. It flies silently with the speed and fluency of a falcon, seizes bats from behind and then swallows them whole in flight, a process facilitated by another adaptation, the very large gape. In one series of observations a Bat Hawk captured an average of seven bats in an eighteen-minute feeding spell each evening. The Bat Hawk lays a single large egg, an aspect of its biology that is probably linked to the limited period during which it can catch food for its chick.

1 Cuckoo Hawk: adult
2 Cuckoo Hawk: juvenile
3 Black-shouldered Kite: adult
4 Black-shouldered Kite: juvenile
5 Bat Hawk: adult
6 Bat Hawk: juvenile
7 Honey Buzzard: pale form
8 Honey Buzzard: dark form
9 Honey Buzzard: barred form
10 Black Kite: adult
11 Black Kite: juvenile
12 Yellow-billed Kite: adult
13 Yellow-billed Kite: juvenile

G G Arnott

17 TAWNY, STEPPE, LESSER SPOTTED, WAHLBERG'S AND BOOTED EAGLES

An assembly of brown eagles such as this is enough to deter the potential raptor enthusiast from continuing further. Identification is indeed initially daunting, especially when the birds are perched, but with practice the distinct differences may be learnt. In flight (see text on next page) the characteristic shape of each species helps to distinguish them.

Except for the Tawny Eagle which may make local movements, all the species shown here are migratory, some from the Palaearctic while others are intra-African. The Tawny Eagle is a common, widespread and highly successful species in Africa. It is a rapacious predator and accomplished pirate but it also obtains much of its food by scavenging, a habit that has resulted, as with the Bateleur, in a marked contraction of its range in southern Africa because of poisoning.

The Steppe Eagle, a Palaearctic migrant to Africa, is often treated as conspecific with the Tawny Eagle. In southern Africa the two are traditionally treated as separate species, which is both logical and convenient, because there are very marked differences in behaviour. The Steppe Eagle is a summer visitor to southern Africa and follows the rain fronts to feed on emerging termite alates, its main food here, although it has a mainly mammalian diet in Russia. It occurs in large numbers, sometimes in company with Lesser Spotted Eagles, but its movements are not well understood. It seems so closely linked to following rain fronts that there is no discernible annual pattern, so its movements need to be constantly monitored. Possibly satellite tracking of marked birds may provide some answers, if this can be achieved.

Wahlberg's Eagle, named after a Swedish naturalist and explorer killed by an elephant in Bechuanaland (Botswana) in 1856, is an intra-African migrant. It is one of the commonest eagles in southern Africa during summer when it breeds. Its migratory movements are poorly understood, but it appears that birds breeding in the south "leapfrog" breeding populations in the north, for example in East Africa. A versatile and rapacious predator, it feeds on a wide spectrum of prey. Although not thought to be a scavenger, cases of poisoning have been reported and have been linked to a population decline in areas of the Transvaal, an alarming recent development.

The Booted Eagle, a small and dashing species, has provided a few surprises for ornithologists. Originally thought to be solely a Palaearctic migrant to southern Africa, it was discovered breeding in the Cape Province in 1973. Since then it has been found to be a common and widespread summer-breeding visitor (August-March) to the Cape Province which moves northwards, mainly to Namibia, in the non-breeding season. In view of the presence of this substantial southern African breeding population, it is now very difficult to distinguish between these birds and Palaearctic migrants, and the extent to which the latter visit our area. The issue is further complicated by the recent discovery of a small breeding population in northern Namibia which breeds in winter!

1 Wahlberg's Eagle: dark brown plumage
2 Wahlberg's Eagle: light brown plumage
3 Wahlberg's Eagle: pale form
4 Booted Eagle: dark form
5 Booted Eagle: pale form
6 Booted Eagle: pale form juvenile
7 Lesser Spotted Eagle: juvenile
8 Lesser Spotted Eagle: adult
9 Tawny Eagle: blond plumage
10 Tawny Eagle: uniform tawny plumage
11 Tawny Eagle: juvenile
12 Tawny Eagle: streaky plumaged female
13 Steppe Eagle: adult
14 Steppe Eagle: juvenile

G G Arnott

18 TAWNY, STEPPE, LESSER SPOTTED, WAHLBERG'S, BOOTED AND SNAKE EAGLES

Brown eagles in flight are not as difficult to distinguish as would at first seem to be the case. Once mastered, their distinctive flight outlines serve to identify them, even in their various plumage forms. The Tawny Eagle, for example, has brown, reddish and pale plumages, as well as variants of these. However, the "classic" eagle proportions of the Tawny are diagnostic, and it can really only be confused with the Steppe Eagle and, to a lesser extent, with the Lesser Spotted Eagle. The Steppe Eagle undoubtedly presents problems, but adults are almost always very dark brown, while juveniles and immatures have distinctive white markings on the wings and upper tail coverts. The Lesser Spotted Eagle differs from both in outline.

In flight Wahlberg's Eagle has been likened to two crossed planks, and the lack of indentations in the flight silhouette gives it a rather stiff-winged appearance. The pale form of the Wahlberg's Eagle could be confused with pale Booted Eagles, but the two species have quite different outlines. In both pale and dark plumage forms the Booted Eagle is best identified by the "landing lights", small patches of white at the junction of the wings and body.

The Banded and Southern Banded Snake Eagles are readily separated by their diagnostic tail patterns, and the longer tail of the latter. However, their ranges are virtually mutually exclusive, so the problem of identification should rarely arise. Both species hunt from a perch and, when they fly, their fast shallow wing-beats are characteristic.

The perched Brown Snake Eagle may be mistaken for other brown eagles, but in flight the plain silvery-white wing-feathers and narrow white tail bands distinguish it. There is a possibility of confusion with the juvenile Black-breasted Snake Eagle which is altogether more reddish, has faint bars on the white wing-feathers and a different tail pattern. The adult Black-breasted Snake Eagle could be mistaken for a Martial Eagle, but the latter appears mainly dark below except for a white abdomen in contrast to the snake eagle's predominantly white underparts. Additionally, the Black-breasted Snake Eagle frequently hunts from a hovering position with slowly winnowing wings, which no other eagle does on a regular basis. This emphasises that not only the flight outline but also the mode of flight and hunting behaviour are important aids to identifying birds of prey.

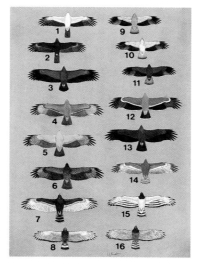

1 Wahlberg's Eagle: pale form
2 Wahlberg's Eagle: brown plumage
3 Lesser Spotted Eagle: adult
4 Tawny Eagle: juvenile
5 Tawny Eagle: blond plumage
6 Tawny Eagle: streaky female
7 Brown Snake Eagle: adult
8 Banded Snake Eagle: adult
9 Booted Eagle: juvenile pale form
10 Booted Eagle: pale form
11 Booted Eagle: dark form
12 Steppe Eagle: juvenile
13 Steppe Eagle: adult
14 Black-breasted Snake Eagle: juvenile
15 Black-breasted Snake Eagle: adult
16 Southern Banded Snake Eagle: adult

G G Arnott

19 BLACK, AFRICAN HAWK, AYRES', LONG-CRESTED, MARTIAL AND CROWNED EAGLES

The Black, Martial and Crowned Eagles are the "big three" of Africa, each impressive in its majesty and power, and each filling a distinct habitat niche. The juvenile plumages of all three are striking, that of the Black Eagle being particularly attractive. The Martial and Crowned Eagle juveniles appear superficially similar but they are easily distinguished in flight (see next plate).

Both Black and Martial Eagles have already been discussed (see pages 46 and 30). The Crowned Eagle is generally considered to be the most powerful of the three and it possesses awesome talons capable of killing a Bushbuck, in one case weighing an estimated 30 kilograms. It is possible in cases such as this that the pair hunt together and combine to overcome their quarry. Large prey is usually dismembered and cached in trees out of reach of predators such as leopards. The Crowned Eagle is primarily a forest eagle but it also occurs in thick woodland, for example in the Matabos Hills in Zimbabwe. Its diet is varied and preferred prey species differ regionally. The principle of "opportunity makes the meal" applies, but usually three categories predominate: small antelopes, monkeys and dassies (hyraxes).

The breeding cycle is a long one with a combined incubation and nestling period of about 160 days and a post-nestling period which may be as long as 350 days. Where a protracted post-nestling period applies the eagles can only breed every second year, a strategy that the late Leslie Brown, the doyen of African raptorphiles, maintained was the norm. The Crowned Eagle was his favourite eagle and his long-term observations were made in Kenya, but it has subsequently been established that Crowned Eagles quite often breed annually, but far less frequently than other African eagles. The Crowned Eagle illustrates that there is always more to be found out, even when a species has been intensively studied.

The African Hawk Eagle and Ayres' Eagle are difficult to distinguish when perched, but in flight there are very marked differences in their underwing patterns (see next plate). Both are dashing species, the African Hawk Eagle preying on gamebirds, small mammals up to the size of a hare and occasional reptiles. The inexplicably rare Ayres' Eagle is one of several birds named after Thomas Ayres', a prominent early South African ornithologist. It is the swiftest of all African eagles and feeds almost exclusively on birds, usually catching them in flight. Recently it has been found to be nomadic, and it is even possible that it is an intra-African migrant.

Another nomadic eagle is the Long-crested Eagle, one species that presents no problems with identification and which, unlike most other African eagles, has no distinct juvenile plumage. It hunts from a prominent perch and may often be seen in the same area day after day as it watches patiently for its mainly rodent prey, particularly vlei rats of the genus *Otomys*. Long-crested Eagles breed erratically and this behaviour is probably linked to the cyclic population changes of the vlei rats.

1 African Hawk Eagle: adult
2 African Hawk Eagle: juvenile
3 Ayres' Eagle: juvenile
4 Ayres' Eagle: adult
5 Long-crested Eagle: adult
6 Martial Eagle: adult
7 Martial Eagle: juvenile
8 Crowned Eagle: juvenile
9 Crowned Eagle: adult
10 Black Eagle: juvenile
11 Black Eagle: adult

BLACK, AFRICAN HAWK, AYRES', LONG-CRESTED, MARTIAL, CROWNED AND AFRICAN FISH EAGLES; BATELEUR AND OSPREY

20

It would be hard to find a more impressive assembly of birds of prey than those depicted here. The flight outline of a bird of prey gives a good indication of how it lives; for example the relatively short broad wings and long tail of the Crowned Eagle enable it to manoeuvre in its enclosed forest habitat, while the longer wings and shorter tail of the Martial Eagle equip it for soaring high above its bushveld environment as it watches for prey far below. The flying skills of the Black Eagle and Bateleur have previously been discussed (pp. 46 and 48), but the longer tail of the juvenile Bateleur should be noted. It projects five centimetres beyond the feet, whereas in the adult the feet project beyond the tail. A number of juvenile raptors have longer tails than the adults and it is thought that this gives them greater stability during the period when they are acquiring their flying skills. As the immature Bateleur progresses to adulthood the tail becomes shorter and it is level with the feet at about two to three years old. This is not the only change, and during its long eight-year transition to adulthood four distinct stages are discernible. At about four years old subadults can be sexed by the amount of black on the trailing edge of the wing. Remarkably, this very obvious distinction between the sexes was overlooked by early ornithologists.

Except for the Martial Eagle which takes six to seven years, no other African eagle has nearly as long a transition from juvenile to adult plumage as the Bateleur; most shown here take three to four years, even the Black and Crowned Eagles. The Long-crested Eagle, however, has no distinctive juvenile plumage.

The various plumage changes during the transition to adulthood inevitably mean that for some eagles many of the intermediate plumage forms can confuse the observer. Of course certain species such as the Black Eagle and Bateleur have such characteristic shapes that they can not be mistaken for anything else. But in the case of others the observer needs to interpolate between the juvenile and adult plumages shown here as it would be impracticable to attempt to illustrate the many stages.

In difficult cases, such aspects as habitat, hunting techniques and mode of flight are useful aids. The Osprey and juvenile African Fish Eagle could conceivably be confused, especially as they occupy the same habitat, but the slow, elastic wing-beats of the Osprey, together with its habit of shaking itself after immersion in pursuit of its quarry, are diagnostic. An African Hawk Eagle would never chase a bird at breakneck speed as it zigzagged through the branches of a tree – an Ayres' Eagle would!

The blotched underparts of the perched Crowned Eagle give it perfect camouflage in the dappled light of its forest environment as it watches for its prey. Why then does it reveal so much white on its wings and tail in flight? The answer would seem to lie in its need to be as conspicuous as possible during undulating display flights to advertise its territory above the forest canopy.

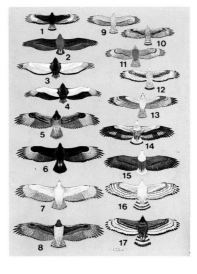

1 Long-crested Eagle
2 Bateleur: juvenile
3 Bateleur: adult female
4 Bateleur: adult male
5 Black Eagle: juvenile
6 Black Eagle: adult
7 Martial Eagle: juvenile
8 Martial Eagle: adult
9 Ayres' Eagle: juvenile
10 Ayres' Eagle: adult
11 African Hawk Eagle: juvenile
12 African Hawk Eagle: adult
13 Osprey
14 African Fish Eagle: juvenile
15 African Fish Eagle: adult
16 Crowned Eagle: juvenile
17 Crowned Eagle: adult

G. G. Arnott

21 SNAKE EAGLES, AFRICAN FISH EAGLE AND OSPREY

The species depicted on this plate are all specialists and serve as a good example of the phenomenon of convergent evolution, in which creatures that are not related, or only distantly, have evolved similar characteristics. In this case the convergence came about because they fed on similar food and in effect illustrates how feeding shapes the bird. The African Fish Eagle and Osprey are both fish-eating specialists, the latter more so, and both have long curved claws and roughened, spiny soles to their feet which enable them to grasp their slippery quarry. However, there the similarity ends, and the two species belong not to different genera but to different families.

The snake eagles are amongst the most interesting of all eagles. There was a time when they were known as harrier eagles, but this unsuitable name has long since been dropped, and the name snake eagle is both descriptive and apt. In the Palaearctic region the single species that occurs there is known as the Short-toed Eagle, a name that draws attention to the small – but immensely strong – feet and short claws of these eagles. Like the African Fish Eagle and Osprey the soles of the feet are rough and spiny, and the scales of the bare legs are thick. These adaptations enable them to grasp and crush snakes and afford protection against the fangs of their quarry. The power and effectiveness of these snake-catching feet are best illustrated by the largest known kill on record – a Black Mamba measuring 2,8 metres killed by a Brown Snake Eagle in Zambia.

The biology of two of the four snake eagles depicted here is poorly known, especially their breeding biology. The Banded Snake Eagle, often called the Western Banded Snake Eagle, is widely distributed in Africa south of the Sahara to northern Botswana and its distribution is by no means "western". Likewise, the Southern Banded Snake Eagle, although it occurs as far south as Zululand, is also found northwards to Kenya, so "southern" is inappropriate. Indeed, as its distribution is confined to the eastern littoral of Africa, it could more accurately be termed "eastern". Both species are in need of more suitable names. Little more than basic information is available on the breeding habits of these two species and any opportunity to study them should not be missed.

Snake eagles have interesting breeding habits and build very small well-concealed nests, so well concealed in fact that few people have studied them. The single large egg has a relatively long incubation period and, once hatched, the nestling rapidly develops a covering of feathers on its head and back so that after a few weeks it can be left alone on the nest while both parents hunt. It is able to swallow prodigious meals whole, for example a large Puff-adder in the case of a Brown Snake Eagle nestling.

Interestingly, the nestling development and other aspects of the biology of snake eagles and the Bateleur are very similar, and in this case it is probable that they are genuinely closely related.

1 Brown Snake Eagle: adult
2 Banded Snake Eagle: adult
3 Southern Banded Snake Eagle: adult
4 Black-breasted Snake Eagle: adult
5 Black-breasted Snake Eagle: juvenile
6 African Fish Eagle: adult
7 African Fish Eagle: juvenile
8 Osprey

22 BUZZARDS

"If you have tears, prepare to shed them now." The Steppe and Forest Buzzards are arguably the most difficult of all our birds of prey to identify. The problem lies in the variability of their plumages and, in the case of the Steppe Buzzard, I have previously coined the name "fingerprint buzzard" for no two are alike. The plate illustrates just how confusing these two species are and, although the Steppe Buzzard is a summer visitor from the Palaearctic and frequents mostly open country, one cannot identify it on this basis alone as it often overlaps the forest-edge habitat of the Forest Buzzard.

The immatures of both these buzzards may be distinguished from adults by their pale biscuit-coloured eyes and by the lack of a broad terminal bar to the tail; these features show up well on 3 opposite. But when it comes to separating immature Forest and Steppe Buzzards from each other, that is another matter! It is now generally accepted that this is almost impossible in the field and they can only be reliably identified in the hand by taking measurements. With adults separation is possible. Dark birds as in 5 opposite are always Steppe Buzzards. If there is horizontal barring on the abdomen then the bird is a Steppe Buzzard because Forest Buzzards are blotched. Although the latter usually have a broad white band on the underparts, the variability in plumage renders this an unreliable feature on its own.

The Forest Buzzard was until recently known as the Mountain Buzzard, but its forest-edge habitat makes its new name far more apposite. If any species should be called Mountain Buzzard on the basis of habitat, then it would be the Jackal Buzzard. Not only has the Forest Buzzard's common name been changed – over a long period its taxonomic position has ranged back and forth more like a shuttlecock than a bird! It is doubtful whether we have heard the last word on the taxonomy of this species.

Both Steppe and Forest Buzzards hunt by patient observation from a perch and feed mainly on small prey such as moles, rodents and insects. There is little detailed information on the prey of either species and further study of their diet would be rewarding. It is only recently that the breeding biology of the Forest Buzzard has been studied in any detail. In one area of the Cape Province pine plantations were preferred for nesting, but always where there was some indigenous forest nearby. Tree-felling during the breeding season may cause nests to be lost, as happened to two out of eight nests in one study.

The Augur Buzzard takes its name from religious officials in Ancient Rome who interpreted omens; presumably its white underparts are reminiscent of the white robes of the augurs. It is a handsome species which has similar habits to the Jackal Buzzard (see p. 34) and with which it is often considered to be conspecific. Its biology is well known, mainly as a result of a study in the Matobo Hills in Zimbabwe where it is common.

1 Forest Buzzard: juvenile
2 Forest Buzzard: adult
3 Steppe Buzzard: juvenile
4 Steppe Buzzard: adult with distinct gorget
5 Steppe Buzzard: adult in dark plumage
6 Steppe Buzzard: adult with reddish blotched plumage
7 Augur Buzzard: juvenile
8 Augur Buzzard: adult male
9 Jackal Buzzard: juvenile
10 Jackal Buzzard: adult

G G Arnott

23 KITES, BAT HAWK, BUZZARDS AND GYMNOGENE

The difficulties in identifying Steppe and Forest Buzzards when perched are not alleviated when they are in flight. The basic pattern of black wing tips, narrow dark trailing edge to the wings and brownish underwing coverts are common to both. The terminal tail band of both species, lacking in immatures, enables them to be identified as adults, and if details of barring on the abdomen can be seen, as in 12 opposite, then it is a Steppe Buzzard.

The Honey Buzzard has a confusing variety of plumages, but the three basic types are shown on Plate 16. The underwing markings are variable, but whatever their colour form the best way to identify them is by the diagnostic tail pattern which has two bars close together near the base of the tail and another near the tip. Juveniles have four evenly distributed bars on the tail. Another useful feature to look for is the small, pointed head which projects well forward of the leading edge of the wings.

Adult Jackal and Augur Buzzards are rarely confused with other species, except that the Jackal Buzzard has superficial similarities to the Bateleur and the Augur Buzzard could possibly be mistaken for a Black-breasted Snake Eagle, but the short red tail of the Augur Buzzard should immediately distinguish it. The black "comma" marks at the carpal joints on the wings are also useful in identifying Augur Buzzards. If perched Jackal Buzzards of the white-breasted form are encountered, it is important to note the underwing pattern so as not to mistake them for Augur Buzzards.

Black and Yellow-billed Kites are very similar in flight, but usually the yellow bill of the latter can be seen. Juvenile Yellow-billed Kites have black bill tips and the best way to distinguish them from Black Kites is by the lack of white on the head. The uniform brown plumage of both *Milvus* kites may lead to confusion with other brown raptors, but the characteristic buoyant flight, with slow, elastic wing-beats, together with the forked tail which is frequently twisted for steering, serve to distinguish them.

The Bat Hawk and Gymnogene are two highly specialised raptors, and the striking differences in their flight silhouettes reveal how hunting techniques shape the bird. The long wings and falcon-like appearance of the Bat Hawk equip it for fast pursuit of its elusive quarry. In complete contrast the broad wings and tail of the Gymnogene, and its relatively light body weight, enable it to do just the opposite. It flies slowly along and alights from time to time to investigate holes in trees and crevices in cliffs, or flips upside down to hang beneath a weaver's nest and rob it of its contents. During its slow methodical searching it quite often catches roosting bats and thus we have two species which use completely different strategies to feed on the same prey.

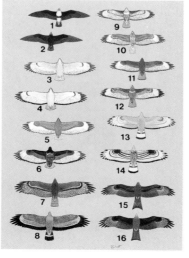

1 Bat Hawk: juvenile
2 Bat Hawk: adult
3 Augur Buzzard: juvenile
4 Augur Buzzard: adult
5 Jackal Buzzard: juvenile
6 Jackal Buzzard: adult
7 Gymnogene: juvenile
8 Gymnogene: adult
9 Forest Buzzard: adult
10 Steppe Buzzard: juvenile
11 Steppe Buzzard: adult in dark plumage
12 Steppe Buzzard: adult with distinct gorget
13 Honey Buzzard: dark form
14 Honey Buzzard: barred plumage
15 Yellow-billed Kite: adult
16 Black Kite: adult

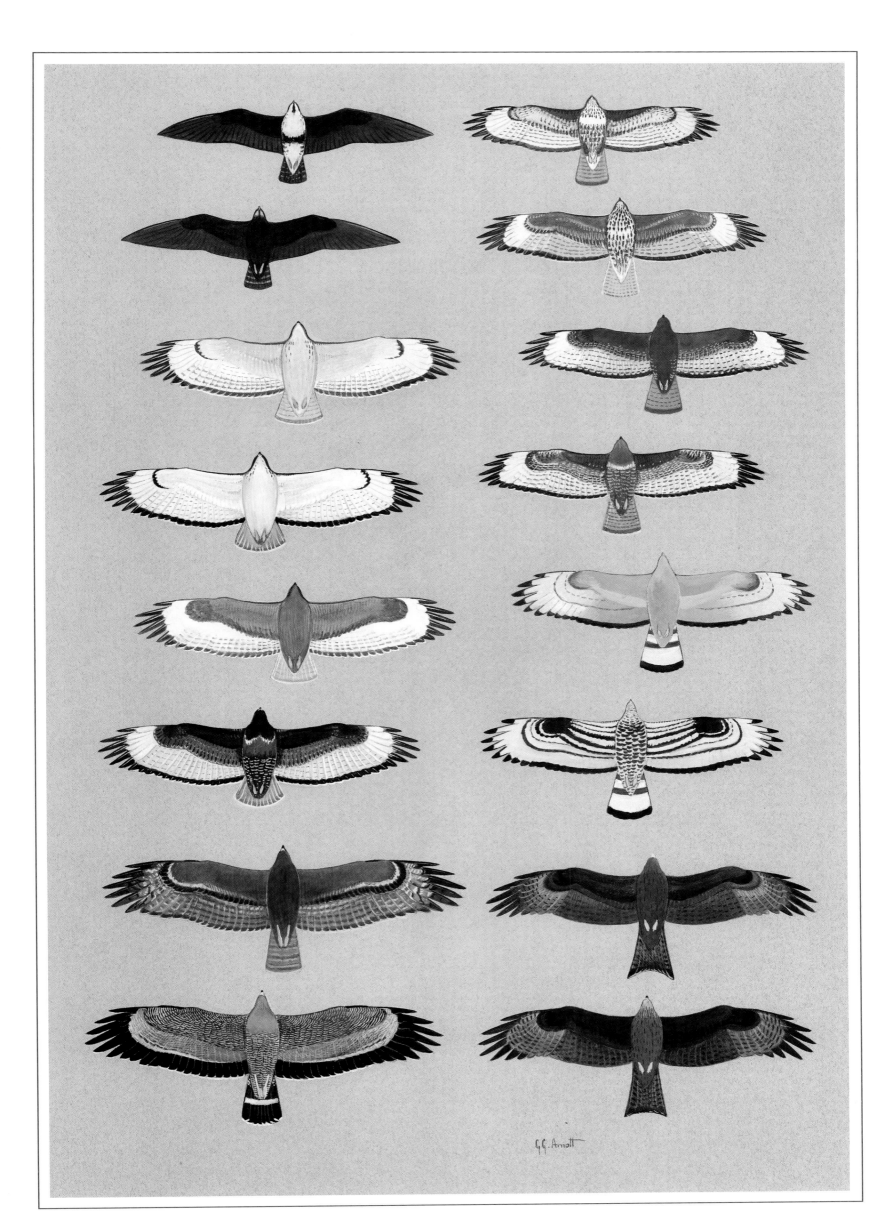

G.G.Arnott

24 SPARROWHAWKS, SMALL GOSHAWKS AND LIZARD BUZZARD

The species shown here include some of the most agile and predatory of Africa's small raptors. The habits of the Ovambo Sparrowhawk are very similar to those of the Red-breasted Sparrowhawk (see p.36), to which it is closely allied, but the two species rarely overlap so do not compete with each other.

The Little Sparrowhawk, the smallest of the African sparrowhawks, is an extremely dashing little hawk that preys mainly on small birds, but also feeds on insects and occasionally on lizards and bats. Its breeding biology is similar to that of other sparrowhawks, but with one unusual feature. Although the normal clutch is two eggs, it is rare for two young to be reared and one usually disappears within a few days of hatching. There is circumstantial evidence of Cainism, but direct observations are needed, especially as such behaviour has not previously been recorded in sparrowhawks.

Very similar in appearance to the Little Sparrowhawk is the Little Banded Goshawk, but it has quite different habits and preys mainly on lizards which are snatched in a quick dash from a perch. It is a common bushveld species and is more likely to be encountered than the secretive Little Sparrowhawk.

The Gabar Goshawk is another widespread and common species, even in relatively arid country. It has all the attributes of an *Accipiter* but is, in fact, a taxonomic enigma traditionally placed in the monotypic genus *Micronisus*. Recent thinking, however, links it to the chanting goshawks which it closely resembles in miniature. Melanistic individuals are not rare and made up 6,5 per cent of a sample of 216 birds in the Kruger National Park. Despite its size it is capable of killing birds as large as a Crested Francolin. It is a highly predatory species with a great turn of speed in pursuit of birds, but it also hunts from a perch and regularly robs nests of their chicks. Small mammals, reptiles and insects are less important components of its diet. A remarkable feature of its nesting behaviour is the deliberate incorporation of nests of the colonial spider of the genus *Stegodyphus* in the early stages of nest construction. As the breeding cycle progresses the nest becomes festooned with cobweb but the function of this unusual behaviour still requires explanation.

The Lizard Buzzard is another taxonomic enigma and is not a true buzzard. In earlier African systematic lists it used to be placed, rather uncomfortably, between the Crowned Eagle and the snake eagles because of a suggested affinity to the latter. Recently it has been proposed that it is more akin to the chanting goshawks with which it shares a similarity in appearance and in the fluting courtship call. As its name correctly indicates, it feeds mainly on lizards, but it also takes snakes, insects and occasionally small mammals and birds. It hunts from a perch in the same manner as a Little Banded Goshawk but is a more robust species and can kill larger prey than the goshawk.

1 Little Sparrowhawk: juvenile
2 Little Sparrowhawk: adult
3 Little Banded Goshawk: juvenile
4 Little Banded Goshawk: adult
5 Red-breasted Sparrowhawk: juvenile
6 Red-breasted Sparrowhawk: adult
7 Gabar Goshawk: juvenile
8 Gabar Goshawk: adult
9 Gabar Goshawk: adult melanistic form
10 Ovambo Sparrowhawk: adult
11 Ovambo Sparrowhawk: juvenile red-breasted form
12 Ovambo Sparrowhawk: juvenile pale-breasted form
13 Ovambo Sparrowhawk: adult melanistic form
14 Lizard Buzzard

G G Arnott

25 BLACK SPARROWHAWK, AFRICAN GOSHAWK, CHANTING GOSHAWKS AND GYMNOGENE

The Black Sparrowhawk is the largest of Africa's sparrowhawks and is an impressive predatory species much prized by falconers. Like a number of other accipiters it has benefited greatly from the spread of alien plantations, particularly eucalypts which are ideal for nesting. In the Transvaal it is estimated that there has been an eightfold increase in the Black Sparrowhawk population in recent times. The availability of roosting and nest-sites in the formerly treeless highveld, together with plentiful prey in nearby cultivated lands, has created optimum conditions for this species.

Doves and pigeons are the preferred prey of the Black Sparrowhawk but it also regularly kills gamebirds up to the size of a guineafowl. Other birds of prey are also included amongst its victims, for example Ovambo Sparrowhawk, Little Banded Goshawk, African Goshawk, Wood Owl and Barn Owl – little wonder that a breeding Black Sparrowhawk usually has the plantation to itself! It is a secretive species which usually catches its prey in flight after a chase launched from cover.

The smaller African Goshawk is also secretive in its habits and could easily be overlooked were it not for its regular soaring territorial displays during which it emits a sharp *whit . . . whit . . . whit* call which carries far. Although it is typically a forest species, it is by no means confined to this habitat and even occurs in well-wooded suburban gardens. It preys mainly on small birds, but also on small mammals, reptiles, amphibians and crabs. The biology of this species is poorly known and merits further study.

The two chanting goshawks shown here are also relatively poorly studied despite being widespread and common. They are ideal subjects for research because they hunt from a conspicuous perch so that colour rings would be easy to see. Prey is normally caught by gliding down from the perch, but both species are capable of a fast dash in pursuit of a bird. The Pale Chanting Goshawk sometimes hunts on foot for short periods, rather like a miniature Secretary Bird. It also regularly follows Honey Badgers and swoops down to snatch anything the badger may disturb as it forages. Interestingly the Dark Chanting Goshawk incorporates the nests of colonial spiders into its nest like the Gabar Goshawk.

The characteristic slow flight of the Gymnogene which equips it for methodical searching has already been discussed (see p. 70). A remarkable adaptation is its double-jointed "knee" which enables it to flex its leg backwards at an angle of 40° for insertion into holes, even woodpecker holes, to extract nestlings or other prey. There is little that escapes the attention of the Gymnogene and it is slight wonder that it is mobbed on sight by other birds. It lays two eggs, beautifully marked, but usually only one chick is reared because Cainism appears to be frequent. Older chicks have been watched as they viciously pecked their siblings to death. The newly hatched chick has long, fine downy plumes on the head, a characteristic shared by chanting goshawk nestlings, and it may be that the Gymnogene may be allied to the chanting goshawks despite its highly specialised adaptations.

1 Black Sparrowhawk: juvenile white-breasted form
2 Black Sparrowhawk: juvenile red-breasted form
3 Black Sparrowhawk: adult
4 Black Sparrowhawk: melanistic form
5 African Goshawk: adult female
6 African Goshawk: juvenile
7 African Goshawk: adult male
8 Dark Chanting Goshawk: juvenile
9 Dark Chanting Goshawk: adult
10 Pale Chanting Goshawk: juvenile
11 Pale Chanting Goshawk: adult
12 Gymnogene: adult
13 Gymnogene: juvenile

26 SPARROWHAWKS, GOSHAWKS, CUCKOO HAWK AND LIZARD BUZZARD

On first impression this array of hawks is intimidating. A major problem is that most of the species shown here share a similar barred pattern on the wings and tail when seen from below. For this reason those on the top half of this plate are illustrated to show their dorsal view because this is where the diagnostic features are apparent.

The best approach is one of systematic elimination beginning with the melanistic forms of the Gabar Goshawk, Ovambo Sparrowhawk and Black Sparrowhawk. The Gabar shows white barring on wings and tail, the Ovambo is plain dorsally except for dark barring on the tail, while the Black Sparrowhawk is uniformly black above and has a white throat.

The adult Little Sparrowhawk and Little Banded Goshawk could easily be confused, but the white rump and "eye" spots on the tail of the former are diagnostic and contrast with the plain dorsal pattern of the Little Banded Goshawk. The juvenile Little Sparrowhawk lacks a white rump but the "eye" spots are still present and the ventral patterns of the juveniles of the two species are quite different (see Plate 24). The juvenile Gabar Goshawk has a similar ventral pattern to the Little Banded Goshawk but its white rump distinguishes it.

The Gabar Goshawk and Lizard Buzzard might be confused because of their similar ventral patterns and white rumps, but the Lizard Buzzard has a diagnostic narrow white bar, occasionally two, near the tip of the tail.

The adult Ovambo Sparrowhawk and Little Banded Goshawk are superficially similar from below but the barring of the former is grey while the Little Banded Goshawk has rufous barring. Dorsally the barred tail of the Ovambo distinguishes it. The Ovambo Sparrowhawk has two juvenile forms and the white-breasted form is shown here. A red-breasted form closely resembles a Red-breasted Sparrowhawk and the two would be difficult to separate in the field. Likewise the Black Sparrowhawk has white-breasted and red-breasted juvenile forms but the much larger size of this species serves to identify them. Mercifully the adult Black Sparrowhawk cannot be confused with anything else!

The adult African Goshawk, especially the smaller male, could be confused with the adult Ovambo Sparrowhawk, Little Sparrowhawk and Little Banded Goshawk. However, the African Goshawk lacks the white rump of the Little Sparrowhawk while its habitat usually helps to separate it from the other two.

The Cuckoo Hawk is placed here because of its similarity to several species on this plate. However, its long wings, from which it derived its former misnomer "Cuckoo Falcon", are diagnostic. It has a fluent graceful flight, but none of the speed of a falcon, and usually plucks its prey from the branches of trees. The juvenile Cuckoo Hawk could easily be mistaken for a juvenile African Goshawk but the wing shape and mode of flight distinguish them; it is possible that the inoffensive Cuckoo Hawk mimics the more predatory African Goshawk and derives a benefit from the similarity.

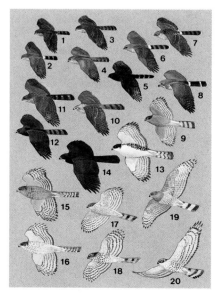

1 Little Sparrowhawk: juvenile
2 Little Sparrowhawk: adult
3 Little Banded Goshawk: juvenile
4 Little Banded Goshawk: adult
5 Gabar Goshawk: adult melanistic form
6 Gabar Goshawk: adult
7 Gabar Goshawk: juvenile
8 Lizard Buzzard
9 Red-breasted Sparrowhawk: adult
10 Ovambo Sparrowhawk: juvenile pale-breasted form
11 Ovambo Sparrowhawk: adult
12 Ovambo Sparrowhawk: adult melanistic form
13 Black Sparrowhawk: adult
14 Black Sparrowhawk: adult melanistic form
15 Black Sparrowhawk: juvenile red-breasted form
16 Black Sparrowhawk: juvenile white-breasted form
17 African Goshawk: adult female
18 African Goshawk: juvenile
19 Cuckoo Hawk: adult
20 Cuckoo Hawk: juvenile

27 HARRIERS

Harriers are attractive birds of prey whose aerial habits make them conspicuous whatever their habitat. Their quartering searching flight is reminiscent of keen-scented harrier dogs hunting for hares and this is almost certainly how their name was derived. In southern Africa five species occur: two residents and three migrants from the Palaearctic region.

As a group harriers are particularly sensitive to environmental degradation, something that has come within my own experience. When I was at school in Cape Town thirty-five years ago African Marsh Harriers were not uncommon on the wetlands of the Cape Flats and during one memorable weekend I was able to find three nests. Now they have almost disappeared as the result of urban sprawl. No species declines in isolation, and the virtual disappearance of the African Marsh Harrier in the environs of Cape Town is indicative of the irreplaceable mosaic of flora and fauna that has gone with it.

When I spent seventeen years in Rhodesia, now Zimbabwe, from 1961 onwards the migrant Montagu's and Pallid Harriers were seen regularly in the grasslands of Matabeleland where I lived. Accepting them as part of the bountiful raptor population there I failed to keep annual counts of their numbers. Only gradually did I become aware that they were steadily disappearing, but by then it was too late to keep records because they had become so rare. Meanwhile, in Kenya, the late Leslie Brown had become aware of a similar decline but was also unable to quantify it.

It seems that habitat alteration resulting from the draining of wetlands and the inexorable expansion of agricultural lands into pristine environments has affected harriers in their Palaearctic breeding range. Inevitably toxic pesticides have been involved, and harriers are also extensively shot, particularly on migration. Paradoxically, in recent years, there have been regular sightings of the formerly rare European Marsh Harrier in southern Africa. Either there has been a real increase in the numbers of this species or greater observer awareness has resulted in more sightings. Incidentally, for a long time the only authentic South African record was a specimen collected in 1869 at Potchefstroom by Thomas Ayres. It has been suggested that the European and African Marsh Harriers are conspecific, but they are so distinct in plumage and size that they are now rarely considered as a single species. Female European Marsh Harriers could be confused with juvenile African Marsh Harriers and careful identification is needed in view of this. Females and juvenile Pallid and Montagu's Harriers are extremely difficult to distinguish from each other, but they can be separated from other brown harriers by their distinctive white rumps.

To conclude on a more positive conservation note, it seems that the handsome endemic Black Harrier (see p. 38) is not presently endangered, although it is essential to monitor its status continuously so that any deterioration may be detected.

1 Montagu's Harrier: adult female
2 Montagu's Harrier: adult male
3 Pallid Harrier: adult male
4 European Marsh Harrier: adult female
5 European Marsh Harrier: adult male
6 Black Harrier: juvenile
7 Black Harrier: adult
8 African Marsh Harrier: juvenile
9 African Marsh Harrier: adult

G G Arnott

28 CHANTING GOSHAWKS AND HARRIERS

The two chanting goshawks shown here are easier to identify in flight than when perched. The adult Pale Chanting Goshawk is altogether a whiter bird and has white secondaries and a conspicuous white rump. The juveniles of the two species are less easy to distinguish but the white rump of the Pale Chanting Goshawk is diagnostic. Although superficially similar to harriers on the wing, the mode of flight of chanting goshawks is quite different with rapid, shallow wing beats interspersed with glides. Their sedentary hunting habits belie the speed of which they are capable at times, and the Pale Chanting Goshawk has been seen to catch birds in flight – in one observation a Harlequin Quail after a 100-metre chase.

Over most of their respective ranges the Pale Chanting Goshawk and Dark Chanting Goshawk do not overlap. Where they do occur contiguously the former is found in more open country and the latter in woodland – a situation which presents an ideal opportunity to study their ecological requirements and the differences, if any, in their feeding habits.

Harriers as a group are characterised by their low quartering flight for which their light weight and long wings and tail are perfect adaptations. *Milvus* kites share similar features but do not use the same methodical low searching flight and have distinctive forked tails which they frequently twist as they steer. The shallow facial disc of harriers which gives them an owlish appearance serves a similar function to that of some owls – to detect sounds in the grass.

While the adult Black Harrier and the males of the Pallid and Montagu's Harrier are easily identified, those harriers which have brown plumage could be misidentified. Females and immatures of both the Pallid and Montagu's Harrier are extremely difficult to distinguish, but they all have white rumps, a feature which separates them from all other brown harriers except for the juvenile Black Harrier which is darker on the head and breast and has a distinct black-and-white tail pattern. The male European Marsh Harrier is a handsome bird with grey upper wings and tail. The female could be mistaken for a juvenile African Marsh Harrier, but she lacks the barring on the wings and tail of that species. Nevertheless, in view of the rarity of the European Marsh Harrier, great care needs to be taken over identification which should be accompanied by field notes made at the time of the sighting. One final pitfall exists – Montagu's Harrier occurs in a rare melanistic form: such a bird could be mistaken for a Black Harrier except that it lacks any white on the rump.

The paucity of resident harrier species in Africa is puzzling. The grasslands provide an ideal habitat and yet no indigenous harrier fills this niche to any extent, allowing migrant harriers to have it to themselves. Sadly, they are seldom seen these days.

1 Pale Chanting Goshawk: juvenile
2 Pale Chanting Goshawk: adult
3 Dark Chanting Goshawk: juvenile
4 Dark Chanting Goshawk: adult
5 Montagu's Harrier: adult male
6 Montagu's Harrier: adult female
7 Pallid Harrier: adult male
8 Black Harrier: juvenile
9 Black Harrier: adult
10 African Marsh Harrier: juvenile
11 African Marsh Harrier: adult
12 European Marsh Harrier: adult female
13 European Marsh Harrier: adult male

29 FALCONS

The falcons shown here include the noblest of all birds of prey: the Peregrine Falcon. The flying skills of this handsome bird are legendary and falconers consider it to have no equal. Small wonder that when the art of falconry was at its peak Peregrines were reserved for the highest levels of the nobility. The Peregrine is a bird-killing specialist capable of considerable speed (see text for Plate 30) and yet, for all its skills, it is a rare species in Africa, perhaps because it is so specialised. The Taita Falcon (see p. 40) is also rare, probably because of competition with Peregrines and Lanner Falcons for cliff nesting-sites.

In the course of a comprehensive survey of the raptors of the Transvaal it was found that breeding pairs of Lanners outnumbered Peregrine pairs eleven to one, and it would seem that a reason for the Peregrine's scarcity may be its need to have high cliffs for hunting and breeding. The Lanner is far more versatile in its hunting techniques and breeding habits and it is probable that the Peregrine cannot compete with it except on its own specialised terms. The Lanner feeds mainly on birds, but also small mammals, reptiles and insects. It also occasionally robs other birds of prey and may even sometimes feed on carrion. Unlike the Peregrine, it is not confined to cliffs for breeding, and lays its eggs in the disused nests of other birds of prey, crows and the like, often on pylons in otherwise unsuitable breeding habitat. As a result the Lanner is the commonest and most widespread of our falcons and may be increasing its range.

The Red-necked Falcon is a dashing species found mainly in the more arid regions of southern Africa, in some areas in association with palms, for example at Makgadikgadi Pan in Botswana. It is also a bird-catching specialist, very swift on the wing, and capable of a rapid rate of climb. Like all falcons the Red-necked Falcon builds no nest and lays in the old stick nests of other birds or in a hollow in a palm where the fronds join the main trunk.

The hobby falcons are extremely fast aerial hunters with a swift-like silhouette. The European Hobby is a summer migrant to Africa from the Palaearctic and often feeds in mixed flocks with migrant kestrels on termite alates which seem to be their main food in Africa. It preys on swallows coming in to roost and also catches swifts. The African Hobby is rare in the southern part of its African range and may be an intra-African migrant; it has been recorded breeding in Zimbabwe. Its biology is little known and it would be a delightful species to study should an opportunity arise.

The exquisite Pygmy Falcon is so small that it could easily be mistaken for a shrike. Unusually, the female is more colourful with her red back which she displays to the male by adopting a submissive posture accompanied by tail-wagging. Its range in southern Africa is mainly in the arid west, where it exactly coincides with that of the Sociable Weaver, and it breeds in the communal nests of this species.

1 African Hobby: juvenile
2 African Hobby: adult
3 Pygmy Falcon: adult male
4 Pygmy Falcon: adult female
5 Red-necked Falcon: adult
6 Red-necked Falcon: juvenile
7 Taita Falcon: adult
8 European Hobby: adult
9 Lanner: juvenile
10 Lanner: adult
11 Peregrine: juvenile
12 Peregrine: adult

30 FALCONS AND GREY KESTREL

The Peregrine normally kills in a spectacular stoop with folded wings and strikes its victim with its hind claws. When it is over, all that is left of the dramatic event is a trail of feathers floating down on the wind. The speed at which a Peregrine stoops has been the subject of much exaggeration and controversy, and in any event the falcon would probably not strike its prey at maximum velocity for fear of injuring itself.

Most estimates of the speed of a Peregrine's stoop range from 150 to 400 kilometres per hour. Falconers in Scotland attached a small air speedometer to a falcon and found that it achieved speeds of some 100 kilometres per hour in level chase and a maximum of 145 kilometres per hour in a stoop. A researcher in Zimbabwe calculated the speed of a number of stoops and found that they averaged 370 with a maximum of 453 kilometres per hour. Even allowing for a fair margin of error in the calculations, it is evident that the Peregrine can stoop at an almost incredible speed. One has only to watch a trained bird in pursuit of quarry to appreciate that the Peregrine is the Ferrari of falcons!

Aerodynamically the Lanner Falcon is less stocky than the Peregrine and has longer wings and tail. Its hunting abilities and speed only suffer comparison with the Peregrine in relative terms; it is an impressive species that is more given to level chase and "binding" to its quarry, a term used by falconers for this method of capture.

Juveniles of the Peregrine and Lanner could be confused but the latter appears much paler on the body and has a rufous "bar mitzvah cap" on the crown in contrast to the uniformly dark head of the Peregrine. The juvenile European Hobby has a superficial resemblance to the juvenile Peregrine but has a much slimmer, swift-like silhouette and its habits are quite different.

Other possible confusions could be between the Taita Falcon and African Hobby, but the stocky build of the former, as well as habits and habitat, serve to distinguish it. The adult Sooty Falcon and Grey Kestrel could easily be misidentified, but the latter has a stockier build and barring on the underwings and tail. Although the Sooty Falcon was originally thought to be confined to the extreme eastern part of southern Africa from Natal northwards, there have been recent random records over a much wider area. Thus, although the Grey Kestrel is found in southern Africa only in the extreme north of Namibia, Sooty Falcons could possibly occur there too.

The Sooty Falcon has fascinating habits. In its breeding range it is found in the eastern Sahara, Sudan, Somalia and the islands of the Red Sea. It migrates mainly to Madagascar and the eastern littoral of Africa. The breeding season is late and is timed so that it can prey on migrants moving southwards. It nests in inhospitable places such as rocky islands in the Red Sea or even in the Sahara where one nest in the shade under a cairn experienced temperatures of 42 °Celsius!

1 Grey Kestrel
2 Sooty Falcon: adult
3 Sooty Falcon: juvenile
4 African Hobby: juvenile
5 African Hobby: adult
6 Taita Falcon: adult
7 European Hobby: juvenile
8 European Hobby: adult
9 Red-necked Falcon: juvenile
10 Red-necked Falcon: adult
11 Lanner: juvenile
12 Lanner: adult
13 Peregrine: adult
14 Peregrine: juvenile

31 KESTRELS AND FALCONS

Of the eight species shown here the Grey, Dickinson's, Rock and Greater Kestrels are resident in Africa. The Rock Kestrel is an African subspecies of the Common Kestrel of the Palaearctic and has traditionally been known as the Rock Kestrel in our region. Unlike the common Kestrel, males and females are not markedly dimorphic and indeed it is somewhat difficult to distinguish the sexes in the field. Despite being widespread and common, its biology has been little studied and any research would prove rewarding. Although usually found in or near mountainous country, it also occurs in featureless arid areas, for example in Botswana and Namibia.

The Greater Kestrel is essentially a species of open country with relatively short cover and is widespread in arid regions. In contrast to the Rock Kestrel it has been relatively well studied, especially its feeding habits. One sample of 1 041 prey items collected from pellets comprised mainly invertebrate prey, mostly orthopterans (crickets and their relatives), and the less than 10 per cent composed of vertebrate prey was recorded mainly during the breeding season.

The Grey Kestrel and Sooty Falcon are more easily distinguished in flight (see text for previous page), but the former is altogether more stockily built with a heavy parrot-like bill and lacks the black "moustache" streak of the Sooty Falcon. Dickinson's Kestrel is pale grey, almost whitish, on the head and upper back, and has a white rump and barred tail. While the breeding biology of the Grey Kestrel is little known, Dickinson's Kestrel has been quite well studied in Zambia; it nests mainly in holes in the trunks of trees, usually palms, but also inside the nests of Hamerkops.

The migrant Western and Eastern Red-footed Falcons visit Africa in large flocks. As their names indicate, the two species occupy western and eastern ranges in the Palaearctic and do not overlap. In southern Africa this separation applies to an extent with the Western Red-footed Falcon, by far the less common of the two, being found mainly in the more arid west. However, the two species not infrequently overlap and even roost together. The Eastern Red-footed Falcon breeds in eastern Siberia, Manchuria and northern China and has an interesting migration pattern. On its route to Africa it travels via north-west India and then 3 000 kilometres over the Indian Ocean. Its northward journey remains a mystery; although it passes through Kenya in April, it does not go back via India and it remains to be established by what route it returns.

The Lesser Kestrel also visits Africa in large numbers and may share roosts with the Western and Eastern Red-footed Falcons. Some roosts have been in use for very long periods and the birds are protected by sentiment because of their value in consuming innumerable insects. Sadly, it appears that these useful summer visitors are declining and some former traditional roosts are no longer in use. The decline is probably due to a number of factors at both ends of their range.

1 Dickinson's Kestrel: adult
2 Western Red-footed Falcon: adult male
3 Western Red-footed Falcon: adult female
4 Sooty Falcon: adult
5 Sooty Falcon: juvenile
6 Eastern Red-footed Falcon: adult male
7 Eastern Red-footed Falcon: adult female
8 Greater Kestrel: adult
9 Grey Kestrel
10 Lesser Kestrel: adult female
11 Lesser Kestrel: adult male
12 Rock Kestrel: adult male
13 Rock Kestrel: juvenile

G G Arnott

32 KESTRELS, FALCONS AND BLACK-SHOULDERED KITE

The Black-shouldered Kite is probably the most visible of all our birds of prey because it perches prominently and hovers frequently. Mention has been made of the relative energetics of these two hunting techniques (see p. 56), the result of fascinating original research. Because it is so conspicuous the Black-shouldered Kite is easy to mark and keep under surveillance; this has revealed unexpected aspects of its biology, for example the regular turnover of individuals in what appears to be a resident population.

The migrant falcons and kestrels shown here are all highly aerial in their hunting techniques and feed in flight on insects, or drop down to snatch grasshoppers off the ground. Where roosts are situated in well-lit country towns the birds will hawk nocturnal insects too. The males of the Western and Eastern Red-footed Falcons are easily distinguished from one another in flight by the white underwing coverts of the latter and the females are also distinctly different.

Dickinson's Kestrel is named after Dr. John Dickinson who was a member of David Livingstone's ill-fated Shiré River expedition in 1861. Its pale head, white rump and barred tail render it easy to identify. It hunts from a perch and drops down on to prey, but it may also dash out and snatch a passing bird in flight. It is attracted to fires where it hovers above the smoke and swoops down to catch birds and insects in flight. Insects are an important component of its diet, but it also preys on small rodents, bats, lizards, chamaeleons, frogs and the occasional small snake. It is altogether a versatile and attractive little raptor.

The juvenile Greater Kestrel can be distinguished from the adult by its reddish, not grey, tail. If a good view is obtained it has a dark eye whereas that of the adult is pale. No other African kestrel or falcon has a pale eye and it is sometimes known by an alternative name as the White-eyed Kestrel. The female Lesser Kestrel and juvenile Rock and Greater Kestrels are all superficially similar. The Greater Kestrel lacks a distinct dark terminal tail band, and the female Lesser Kestrel differs from the Rock Kestrel in being much paler in colour with streaking, not spotting, on the underparts.

The Pygmy Falcon has a fast, dipping flight like that of a Pearl-spotted Owl. It hunts from a perch and drops down on to prey or makes a quick dash at a passing bird. Prey comprises mainly insects and lizards, the latter being an important part of the diet during the breeding season. Rodents and birds are also occasionally caught. The Pygmy Falcon breeds in a nest chamber of a Sociable Weaver's nest and, although abandoned structures may be used, the little falcon usually occupies a nest chamber alongside the weavers in apparent amity. Once the chicks hatch a ring of hardened white droppings round the entrance to the nest indicates its occupancy by the falcons.

1 Western Red-footed Falcon: adult male
2 Western Red-footed Falcon: adult female
3 Eastern Red-footed Falcon: adult male
4 Eastern Red-footed Falcon: adult female
5 Pygmy Falcon: adult male
6 Pygmy Falcon: adult female
7 Dickinson's Kestrel
8 Lesser Kestrel: adult male
9 Lesser Kestrel: adult female
10 Black-shouldered Kite: adult
11 Rock Kestrel: juvenile
12 Rock Kestrel: adult
13 Greater Kestrel: adult
14 Greater Kestrel: juvenile

33 BARRED, PEARL-SPOTTED, AFRICAN SCOPS, WHITE-FACED, WOOD AND MARSH OWLS

It would be hard to find a more appealing group of owls than those depicted here. The Barred and Pearl-spotted Owl form a species pair and belong to the genus *Glaucidium* whose name is derived from the Greek *Glaukidion* meaning "small owl". The perky, almost elfin, appearance of both species makes them particularly attractive, and their calls, particularly that of the Pearl-spotted Owl, enhance many a camper's experience of the African night. The African Scops Owl and White-faced Owl form another species pair in the genus *Otus*. Although superficially similar, they are markedly different in size and roosting behaviour and should not be confused. The African Scops Owl is a master of camouflage and roosts against the bark of a tree-trunk where it is all but invisible. If danger threatens it closes its eyes to slits and elongates its body to resemble an emaciated Chinese idol. Usually the first evidence of its presence in an area is at dusk when its insect-like ventriloquial *prrrup* call is repeated at short, regular intervals, but trying to locate its position with a flashlight is another matter! The White-faced Owl does not conceal itself particularly well, but if disturbed also elongates its body and ear tufts to make its disruptive camouflage more effective. The White-faced Owl's call is a lovely bubbling hoot, quite different from that of the African Scops Owl, but if disturbed at the nest it emits an extraordinary cat-like snarling. The White-faced Owl lays its eggs in hollows in trees or on the disused nests of other birds, even the flimsy stick nest of a Grey Lourie. This has given rise to erroneous reports that it builds a nest, although no owl is known to do so. The African Scops Owl nests in small holes in trees, usually open at the top, and sits extremely tight with its face down if the nest is inspected. Recently, in Namibia, this species used nest-boxes placed for other hole-nesting birds enabling its previously poorly known breeding biology to be studied in some detail. Although the African Scops Owl was previously thought to be exclusively insectivorous, the Namibian observations revealed that it also preys on lizards and the occasional small mammal.

The Wood Owl and Marsh Owl belong to completely different genera and almost the only thing they have in common is their dark eyes. Why the eyes of some owls are dark and others yellow or orange is something that remains to be adequately explained; certainly it has nothing to do with visual acuity, but pale eyes may serve a threat or display function. The Wood Owl is southern Africa's only true forest owl, although it is by no means confined to this habitat. Its melodious hooting calls are quite delightful. In contrast, the Marsh Owl, which lives in moist open grassland, emits a harsh croaking call. It is the nocturnal counterpart of the African Marsh Harrier, but may emerge on dull days to hunt, when both species can be seen together.

1 Barred Owl
2 African Scops Owl
3 White-faced Owl
4 Pearl-spotted Owl
5 Wood Owl
6 Marsh Owl

34 BARN AND GRASS OWLS, EAGLE OWLS, PEL'S FISHING OWL

The Barn and Grass Owls form a species pair in the genus *Tyto* (from the Greek *tuto*, a night owl). As may readily be seen from the plate they are distinctly different from other owls. The heart-shaped facial disc and long legs are two obvious features, but they also have several skeletal differences. One view even holds that they are more closely related to falcons than to other owls.

The Barn Owl is the most widely distributed of the world's land birds and thirty-five races are recognised. It is a species with fascinating habits, the most remarkable of which is its ability to catch prey in total darkness using its hearing alone. The African race of the Barn Owl is widely distributed and does not appear to be endangered, unlike its grassland counterpart the Grass Owl which has suffered from the degradation of its habitat as a result of draining, too frequent fires and overgrazing. The biology of the Barn Owl has been well studied in a number of localities in Africa, but that of the Grass Owl requires detailed investigation.

The three eagle owls shown here are all "eared" owls, but these ear-tufts have nothing whatsoever to do with hearing and serve as disruptive camouflage and possibly as a recognition signal. The Spotted Eagle Owl is common and widely distributed in southern Africa in a variety of habitats, including towns. Consequently, it is the best-known owl and the most likely "eared" owl to be seen perched beside the road at night.

The Cape Eagle Owl has a wide distribution from the south-west Cape to Ethiopia and three races are recognised. It is an elusive species found in mountainous or rocky terrain and is easily overlooked. The largest race *mackinderi*, often called Mackinder's Eagle Owl (after Sir Halford Mackinder who made the first ascent of Mount Kenya), was only discovered in Zimbabwe in 1967, but since then it has been found to be widely distributed there in suitable habitat. The smaller race *capensis* has recently been found to occur in arid areas of the Karoo and even in Namibia. The Cape Eagle Owl is much more powerful than the Spotted Eagle Owl and kills mammals up to the size of hares.

The Giant Eagle Owl and Pel's Fishing Owl (see p. 44 for text on the latter) are amongst the largest of the African owls. The Giant Eagle Owl is very powerful and has been well described as an omnivorous nocturnal butcher. Its spectrum of recorded prey ranges from items as small as insects and white-eyes to a Warthog piglet or roosting Secretary Bird! Although the other eagle owls have pleasant hooting calls, that of the Giant Eagle Owl is a series of deep dyspeptic grunts. The young owl makes a high-pitched ventriloquial whistling call that carries far. In common with other young owls a distinctive begging call enables the parents to locate their young once they have left the nest.

1 Spotted Eagle Owl
2 Barn Owl
3 Pel's Fishing Owl
4 Grass Owl
5 Cape Eagle Owl
6 Giant Eagle Owl

BIBLIOGRAPHY

GENERAL REFERENCES

The following references were used throughout the text, or for the introductory chapters.

ALLAN, D.G. 1989. Strychnine poison and the conservation of avian scavengers in the Karoo, South Africa. *South African Journal of Wildlife Research* 19(3):102-106.
AMADON, D., BULL, J., MARSHALL, J.T. & KING, B.F. 1988. Hawks and owls of the world: a distributional and taxonomic list. *Western Foundation of Vertebrate Zoology* 3(4):295-397.
ANON. EDITOR. 1985. A matter of trust. *Honeyguide* 31(2):76-77.
BROOKE, R.K. 1984. South African Red Data Book – Birds. *South African National Scientific Programmes Report* No. 97. Council for Scientific and Industrial Research, Pretoria.
BROWN, L. 1970. *African birds of prey.* Collins, London.
BROWN, L.H., URBAN, E.K. & NEWMAN, K. 1982. *The birds of Africa.* Vol. 1. Academic Press, London.
FINCH-DAVIES, C.G. & KEMP, A. 1980. *The birds of prey of southern Africa.* Winchester Press, Johannesburg.
FRY, C.H., KEITH, S. & URBAN, E.K. 1988. *The birds of Africa.* Vol. 3. Academic Press, London.
HARTLEY, R. 1988. Conservation activities of the Zimbabwe Falconers' Club. *Bokmakierie* 40(1):15-17.
SIEGFRIED, W.R. 1984. Red data books: Bibles for protectionists, Aunt Sallies for conservationists. In Mundy, P.J. (ed.): *Proceedings of an International Symposium on the Extinction Alternative* pp. 119-126. Endangered Wildlife Trust, Johannesburg.
STEYN, P. 1973. *Eagle days.* Purnell, Johannesburg.
STEYN, P. 1982. *Birds of prey of southern Africa.* David Philip, Cape Town.
STEYN, P. 1984. *A delight of owls.* David Philip, Cape Town.
TARBOTON, W.R. & ALLAN, D.G. 1984. The status and conservation of birds of prey in the Transvaal. *Transvaal Museum Monograph* No. 3. Transvaal Museum, Pretoria.

Additionally, various issues of the following were referred to extensively for conservation information:
Newsletters of the World Working Group on Birds of Prey and Owls (printed in Germany) and *Vulture News* (printed in Johannesburg).

SPECIFIC REFERENCES

These references are relevant to the texts which appear opposite the various plates.

Plate 1: BROWN, C.J. 1988. A study of the Bearded Vulture *Gypaetus barbatus* in southern Africa. Unpublished Ph.D. thesis. University of Natal, Pietermaritzburg.

Plate 2: ROBERTSON, A.S. & BOSHOFF, A.F. 1986. The feeding ecology of Cape Vultures *Gyps coprotheres* in a stock-farming area. *Biological Conservation* 35:63-86.

Plate 3: BOSHOFF, A. 1986. Stability of a population of Martial Eagles in a sheep farming area in the Great Karoo South Africa: project outline and early results. *Gabar* 1(1):9-13.
HUSTLER, K. & HOWELLS, W.W. 1987. Breeding periodicity, productivity and conservation of the Martial Eagle. *Ostrich* 58(3):135-138.

HUSTLER, K. 1988. Martial Eagle lays two-egg clutch. *Honeyguide* 34(2):70.
ROOD, J.P. 1983. Banded Mongoose rescues pack member from eagle. *Animal Behaviour* 31(4):1261-1262.

Plate 4: BANDS, M. 1983. Odd snatches. *Diaz Diary* 124:7.
COLLIS, D.J. 1986. Fish Eagle taking avian prey in flight. *Honeyguide* 32(3&4):151.
CULVERWELL, J. 1985. A shoal of Fish Eagles. *African Wildlife* 39(6):248.
HANSEN, A.J. 1985. The Fish Eagle in love or war. *African Wildlife* 39(2):74.
NEWMAN, K. 1980. Notes from Malaŵi. *Bokmakierie* 32(4):122.
NEWMAN, K. 1984. More notes from Malaŵi. *Bokmakierie* 36(2):31-32.
SAUNDERS, C. 1985. Interlocked Fish Eagles. *African Wildlife* 39(6):249.
STEYN, P. 1984. Courtship in the African Fish Eagle. *African Wildlife* 38(3):117.
STEYN, P. 1985. Further observations on the African Fish Eagle. *African Wildlife* 39(6):249.
VAN VUUREN, P.A.J. 1984. Do Fish Eagles eat reptiles? *African Wildlife* 38(1):30.

Plate 5: SCHMITT, M.B., BAUR, S. & VON MALTITZ, F. 1987. Observations on the Jackal Buzzard in the Karoo. *Ostrich* 58(3):97-102.

Plate 6: SIMMONS, R. 1984. Pre-independence behaviour, morphometrics and trapping of fledgling Redbreasted Sparrowhawks. *Ostrich* 55(3):158-162.
SIMMONS, R. 1986. Food provisioning, nestling growth and experimental manipulation of brood size in the African Redbreasted Sparrowhawk *Accipiter rufiventris.* *Ornis Scandinavica* 17:31-40.
SIMMONS, R. 1986. Ecological segregation of the Redbreasted Sparrowhawk *Accipiter rufiventris* and six co-existing accipitrine raptors in southern Africa. *Ardea* 74:137-149.
STEYN, P. 1988. Observations on the Redbreasted Sparrowhawk. *Bokmakierie* 40(3):66-73.

Plate 7: STEYN, P. & MYBURGH, N. 1989. Development halted for a Black Harrier. *Bokmakierie* 41(1):15.
VAN JAARSVELD, J. 1986. Notes on a Black Harrier's nest. *Bokmakierie* 38(3):75.

Plate 8: MÖLLER, P. 1989. The Taita Falcon *Falco fasciinucha*: results of a study at Mt. Elgon. Raptors in the modern world. *Proceedings of the 111 World Conference on Birds of Prey and Owls* pp. 315-319.

Plate 9: BRAYBROOKE, T. 1985. Notes on observations of Barred Owls on Mr Hans Hoheisen's farm "Kempiana", adjacent to Kruger National Park. *Wilderness* 17 (newsletter of the Wilderness Leadership School).
BROOKE, R.K., OATLEY, T.B., HURLEY, M.E. & KURT, D.W. 1983. The South African distribution and status of the nominate race of the Barred Owl. *Ostrich* 54(3):173-174.
CARLYON, J. 1985. Rediscovery of the Barred Owl in the eastern Cape Province. *African Wildlife* 39(1):22-23.
CROUS, R. 1988. Barred Owl kills a snake. *African Wildlife* 42(1):225.

Plate 11: BOSHOFF, A. & FABRICIUS, C. 1986. Black Eagles nesting on man-made structures. *Bokmakierie* 38(3):67-70.
FRASER, M.W. 1985. Black Eagle dropping tortoise. *Promerops* 168:9-10.
LEDGER, J.A. & HOBBS, J. 1987. First record of a Black Eagle nesting on an electricity transmission tower. *African Wildlife* 41(2)60-66.
STEYN, P. 1984. Black Eagles dropping tortoises. *Promerops* 162:12.

Plate 12: WATSON, R.T. 1986. The ecology, biology and population dynamics of the Bateleur Eagle (*Terathopius ecaudatus*). Ph.D. thesis. University of the Witwatersrand, Johannesburg.

Plate 14: BROWN, C.J. 1986. Biology and conservation of the Lappetfaced Vulture in SWA/Namibia. *Vulture News* 16:10-20.

Plate 16: CHITTENDEN, H. 1984. Aspects of Cuckoo Hawk *Aviceda cuculoides* breeding biology. *Proceedings of the 2nd Symposium on African Predatory Birds* pp. 47-56. Natal Bird Club, Durban.
MENDELSOHN, J. 1984. The timing of breeding in Black-shouldered Kites in southern Africa. *Proceedings of the 5th Pan-African Congress* pp. 799-808. Southern African Ornithological Society, Johannesburg.

Plate 17: BROWN, C.J. 1985. Booted Eagles breeding in Namibia. *Madoqua* 14(2):189-191.
CARLYON, J. 1985. Wahlberg's Eagle dies of strychnine poisoning. *African Wildlife* 39(6):239-241.
TARBOTON, W. 1986. Wahlberg's Eagles decline at Nylsvley. *African Wildlife* 40(1):39.

Plate 19: VERNON, C.J. 1984. The breeding periodicity of the Crowned Eagle. *Proceedings of the 2nd Symposium on African Predatory Birds* pp. 125-137. Natal Bird Club, Durban.

Plate 20: WATSON, R.T. 1987. Flight identification of Bateleur age classes: a conservation incentive. *Bokmakierie* 39(2):37-39.

Plate 22: PALMER, N.G., NORTON, P.M. & ROBERTSON, A.S. 1985. Aspects of the biology of the Forest Buzzard. *Ostrich* 56(1,2 & 3):67-73.

Plate 24: COLEBROOK-ROBJENT, J.F.R. 1986. On the validity of the genus *Micronisus*. *Gabar* 1(1):7-8.
KEMP, A.C. 1986. The Gabar Goshawk: taxonomy, ecology and further research. *Gabar* 1(1):4-6.
KEMP, A.C. & RAUTENBACH, I.L. 1987. Bat Hawks or bat-eating hawks? *Gabar* 2(1):4-6.

Plate 29: IRWIN, M.P.S. 1981. *The birds of Zimbabwe.* Quest, Salisbury.

Plate 30: HUSTLER, K. 1983. Breeding biology of the Peregrine Falcon in Zimbabwe. *Ostrich* 54(3):161-171.

Plate 31: KEMP, A.C. & FILMER, M. 1989. The diet of Greater Kestrels *Falco rupicoloides* near Pretoria, South Africa. *Ostrich* 60(2):65-68.

Plate 33: BROWN, C.J., RIEKERT, B.R. & MORSBACH, R.J. 1987. The breeding biology of the African Scops Owl. *Ostrich* 58(2):58-64.

LIST OF SUBSCRIBERS

SPONSORS' EDITION

Peter Adam & Misha Coetzee
Finn & Victoria Allan
Dorothy Judith Barker
Mr & Mrs F.J. Barrell
W.F.L. Blanden
The Brenthurst Library
The Rt Hon. Viscount
 Chetwynd
Ian G. Douglas
Lydia Gorvy
Caitlin Japhet
M.F. Keeley
Dr William Moore
H.M. Peet
M.L.P. Rattray (Mala Mala)
Kathleen Satchwell
Mr & Mrs H.R. Slack
Dr & Mrs Sydney N. Smith
P.A. Stone
Michael J. Vermooten
De Beer Industrial Diamond
 Division (Pty.) Ltd.

COLLECTORS' EDITION

P. Adams
Adams & Company
Africana Book Collectors
G. Angelini
A.J. Ardington
Graeme Arnott
Stephen Bales
Alex A. Barrell
Don Barrell
Mrs D.P. & Mr.S. Baur
Peter Becker
P.A. Becker
Dr & Mrs R.M.F. Berard
Johan & Gardiol Bergenthuin
Ari & Gia Bert
Bevan Family
Iris Binks
Ian, Sue and Kerry-Anne Bishop
Colin R. Blythe–Wood
David K. Bond
Basil Brady
B. Braude
Brightwater, Hohenhort
Jim Gerard Paul Broekhuysen
Mike & Pat Buchel
Piers J.M. Burton-Moore
W.J. Chambers
A.F. Coetzee
Pietro Corgatelli
Dr & Mrs W.R. Cunliffe
Donald & Rosemary Currie
Gerhard Rudolf Damm
Dr & Mrs M.R. Davies
W.H.J. de Beer
Karlien de Bruin
Sandra de Witt
W.R. Doepel
Meryl Fahrenheim
Dr John Fannin
Feathers of Knysna
Peter B. Ferrett
Peter Ford
Malcolm Foster
Eugene & Lalie Fourie
Russel, Bonnie & Gabriella Friedman
Michael, Rosemary, Dean & Lisa Fuller
P.B. Gain
E.S.C. Garner
Rob Gee
Jim Gordon
P.M. Goss
Pinchas & Dorothy Gütter
Manfred, Marie, Irene & Rudolf Hanni
Colin & Hazel Harper
D.A. Hawton
John K. Hepburn
Keith Hepburn
Basil Hersov
Neill W.W. Hester
Margie & Dave Hidden
Chris & Mary Hull
C.R. Hunting
Miss L.-M. Hunting
L.R. Hunting
M.S. Hunting
I. Hussain
M.J. Hyde
R.G. Jeffery
David F. Jenkins
Roger Johnson
Rod & Noreen Kippen
Errol & Freda Kreutzer

Micheline Logan
Johan & Edwina Lombard
C.S. Louw
Helen MacGregor
Cherrie MacKensie
O.J. Mackenzie
Thomas Walter Martin
John Matterson – Bushdrifters
Roxana McCormick
James McLuskie
Mimosa Lodge, Montagu
I.B. Minnaar
Kay & Peter Mitchell
Jan & Elizabeth Nel
Danie, Nita, Daniel & Christiaan
 Olivier
Margaret & David O'Reilly
Robert & Sheila Pickering
Dr & Mrs D.G.C. Presbury
Richard J. Price
F.R. Prinsloo
M. Raath
John Rae
Brenda & Wim Reinders
Rodney K. Reynolds
Geoff & Joan Robin
J.A. Rochford
Dave & Eulah Rosenberg
John & Corinne Roy
Con en Jacqueline Schabort
Sarah Schoeman
R.E. Scholz
Norman Segal
Jennifer Shadrach
Bill & Virginia Sonnenberg
Heidi Sorbrook
June Stannard
Naas Steenkamp
Peter Steyn
Pieter Struik
B.J. Swart
Ian R.F. Trollip
A.C.C. Turner
Mr & Mrs J.J. Turner
G.A. Upfill-Brown
Francois van der Merwe
B.J. van Heerden
H.G. van Heerden
W. van Rÿswÿck
Pieter Wagener
Roy & Lorraine Webber
Peter & Jeffe Williams
Ilse & Stephan Wentzel
Ross Young

STANDARD EDITION

Stanley P. Abramson
D.J.J. Ackermann
Bo Acheson
J.J. Ackermann
Paul H. Adler
Africana Book Collectors
Alexander L.D. Agenbacht
M. Alberts
Simon J.F. Allen
B.W. Alleson
David & Ann Alston
August Altenroxel
Dr Ingram F. Anderson
Mr & Mrs D. J. Anderson
Des & Elizabeth Andersson
Jonathan & Tracey Andrews
Harold Annegarn
A.R.I.C.
N.J. Arkell
E.H. Ashton
H.B. Atherstone
J.D. Austin
Barbara Bailey
Gina Baldo
Roger & Audrey Baldwin
Ian Bales-Smith
Charles Ball
George & Mary Banfield
Pamela Barlow
B. Barnes
M.L. Barnes
Mr & Mrs C. Barrow
Doug & Wendy Barrow
André M.J. Bastenie
David B. Batchelor
M. Batchelor
Dr A.E. Bateman
David & Cathy Bath
Rolf & Rosalie Bathauer
Matthew Beauclerk
Jane Bedford
Frank & Di Beeton
George & Lea Begg
R.H. Behrens
Karena Benade
John & Joan Bennett
Conal Benson
Dr & Mrs R.M.F. Berard
L.M. Berger
Birch Bernstein

R.M. Berry
M.A. Betty
Major J.E. Bishop
Alexander Black
David & Dee Black
Robert Black
Dr & Mrs J.D. Blackburn
Richard & June Blackwell
Cecil & Marian Bleksley
G.P. Bligh
I.A.N. Bloy
Derek Bluck
Theo & Varina Bosman
C.J. Botha
Louis B. Botha
M.C. Botha
Michiel J. Botha
Rudolph Botha
Alan Bowden
J.T. Bowen
William M.D. Bowker
Richard Boyton-Smith
Mary Bradley
Edna & Frank Bradlow
Alison Brand
H.D. & S. Brandt
Dr Andy & Wendy Branfield
Irene Bredenkamp
A.T. Bremner
Patrick & Jenny Brett
C.J. & Honor Breyer-Menke
Willem Breytenbach
David Brierley
Peter Brigg
Alice & Jeandrew Brink
Kay Brinkman
T.H.E.D. Briscoe
A.P. Bristow
R.C. Brooks
A.J.L. Brown
Alexander Brown
Roy & Maureen Brown
Strath Brown
A.P. Browne
Max Bruessow
N.R.G. Brunette
Anton Bryant
H.J. & M.A. Brynard
Neville & Barbara Bucke
Karen Bullen
A. Westley Burman
Bruce W. Burman
Donald Burnett
Rob & Wendy Burnett
Bushwillow
Mr & Mrs I.E. Butler
I.S. Buys
D.R. Calder
Kelson Camp
A.M.A. Campbell
D.B. Campbell
Norman A. Campbell
Doris Ashbourne Cann
Sean & Marta Cannon
Bruce, Clare & Dunstan Cantle
C.R. Carlsen
Peter Carson
Dawn & Chip Cathcart Kay
J.R. Cawood
The Central Bookshop, Blantyre
Gregory Milton Chamberlin
Jean-Paul Chatagnon
Mike Chatkin
Carol & Saj Chaudry
Theo Christensen
William John Clarke
A.C.V. Clarkson
Ted & Estelle Clayson
Mr & Mrs A. Clement-Smith
C.F. Clinning
R.J. Clinton
Derek & Julia Cluver
Jacklyn Cock
Ian D.J. Cochrane-Murray
Deon Coetzee
Johann & Steph Coetzee
Ludwig Coetzer
Des & Naureen Cole
Jean Collier
Dr D.J. Comyn
Dr & Mrs G. Conforzi
Dennis, Palla, Deanne & Anthony
 Coole
M.A. Coombe-Heath
Clive & Sue Cooper
D.E. Cooper
Patty & Coops Cooper
Tracy & Rodney Cooper
George & Mary Coram
Elaine Cormack
Grant Cornish-Bowden
Jagger Cornish-Bowden
Ian & Sylvia Coulson
Paul & Marlene Coulson
Prof. J.L. Couper
Dr Graham Coupland
C.L. Cousins

R. Cowgill
Graham & Jillian Cox
Tony & Leone Cox
John Cranke
R.M. Crawford
Sean Cremen
Elizabeth Crisp
Richard Crocker
N.S. Cronjé
Frans Cronjé
Norman Cross
Percy Croudace
David & Bernice Crouse & Boys
Adam & Rupert Cruise
Jack Crutchley
Kevin H. Culverwell
Malcolm Cumming
Harold H. Currie
Rosemary Curry
Bernard J.L. de Souza
Ian Daniel
Leon R. Daniels
Sean R. Daniels
Samuel C. Dansie
Wade Paul Anthony Darby
Dennis, Jenny, Mandy & Richard
 Da Silva
D.A. Davies
Dr & Mrs M.R. Davies
P. Davies-Webb
Timothy O. Davis
Allen Davson
Chris & Lynn Day
Jim Dayton
Sam & Ralda de Beer
D. & N. Deacon
Hartwig Dedekind
Louis Deenik (Jnr.)
Bertus de Jager
W. de Jager
Hennie & Rina de Klerk
Dr Jan de Kock
Y.E. de Milne-Timmermans
E.B. Denman
A.L. de la Rey
Kevin Deutschmann
Francois de Villiers
Wouter de Vos
William Dewar
Dr Nic de Wet
Leicester Dicey
Claudia Dickson
Peter & Carol Ditz
Cynthia & Denys Dixie
Tony & Mags Dixon
Robert Domijan
Grant Donaldson
Terry Donnelly
Llewellyn, Cecilia, Celést & Werner
 Doubell
P.Dubb
K.W.G. Duff
Graham Dumbrill
Ewan Duncan & Family
Gordon Duncan
Patrick Dunseith
Dunvegan Primary School
Gideon du Plessis
Joyce & René du Plessis
Louis & Neil du Plessis
Willie du Plessis
B.N. du Preez
Francois du Randt
C.J.H. du Toit
Dalene & Fanus du Toit
Henriette du Toit
Rean F. du Toit
Stephen du Toit
André S.F. Eady
Rob Earle
F.G. Eckl
John S.R. Edge
Peter & Brix Edgington
Graham Edkins
E.A. Edwards
Elandsrand Gold Mining
 Company Ltd
Richard Eley
P.R. Eloff
Barry Emberton
R.R. Emmett
D.P. Enright
Felix Ernst
H. Ernst
Eskom
J.D.P. Esterhuizen
Allison Evans
Ian Evans
James & Dominic Evans
Charles H. B. Everard
C.P. & C.J. Everitt
Joe & Gwyn Faller
V.J. Faris
Pauline Farquhar
Professor P.K. Faure
Joan, Matthew & Brendan Fawson
J.M. Feeley

Mr & Mrs A.N. Fernsby
Vital E. Ferry
Khakie Ferreira
Sandra L. Fisher-Jeffes
P.J. Fitt
Douglas Vesey Fitz-Gerald
Margaret Fleming
J.P. Fletcher
Mr & Mrs B. St C. Forbes
Malcolm Foster
Beverley Fourie
D.J. Gain
D.R. Gain
P.K. Gain
R.M. Gain
Alan Galante
Tony Galley
Douglas C. Galpin
John Gardner
H.E. Gearing
Mrs H.M. Geerlings
David Gevisser
Hendrik & Jane Geyer
Barrie & Pam Gibbons
Jonathan M. Gibson
John Gilchrist
K.P. & G.M. Gillespie
Piero Giorgi
A. Girling
H.J.L. Goetsch
Michael Goldblatt
Mr & Mrs J.D. Goodyear
Mel Goott
Adele Gordon
Dr J.M. Gosnell
Nicholas M. Goss
Richard John Goss
A.M. Goulding
K.C. Goulding
Mr & Mrs C. Grabrandt
A.W. Graham
Mike & Les Graham
Norman & Avril Green
Rodney & Sue Green
Tom Gregory
Kobie Greyling
M.J. Greyvensteyn
Gerrie & Margaret Griffioen
Eileen & Cor Grobbelaar
George & Cherry Grobler
Mike Groch
John Groenewald
J.M. Gurney
R.M. Gush
A.C. Hacking
Dawn Haggie
Helen Hahn
Anthony & Bernie Hall
Dorothy G. Hall
R.S. & B.A. Hall
Ken Halliday
Dr Anthony Hall-Martin
Andrew Halstead
Philippa Halstead
Craig Halsted
R.G. Halton
Elize Hamman
Janet M.J. Hammond
Roz Harding
Derek Harraway
Frederick Harrison
James du Guesclin Harrison
J.E. Harrison
Jonathan & Jeanie Harrod
James Hart
David & Tessa Hartley
Henry Hartley
R.A. Harvey
G.G. Havemann
Reneé Hawes
Karen Hawinkels
Jeffrey Hawkes
R.G. Hawkins
J.B. Hawthorne
M.J. Hawthorne
D.A. Hawton
Neil Haybittel
Lisa & Giles Hefer
Mr & Mrs A.M.H. Henley
J.D. Hepburn
John & Beryl Hepburn
Mr & Mrs G.B. Herbert
Kotie Herholdt
Mark J.V. Hewat
Anthony Heyns
Colin C. Hilder
Nigel Hill
R.S. Hislop
H.L. & H. Mining Timber
Terence Hoal
Grant Hobbs
Guy Hodson
N.v.R. Hoets
Robert Holbrook
Craig, Sue, Giles & Alan Holmes
G.R. Holtshausen
Frances Homber

J.F. Home
Diana Hood
Barbara & Owen Hooker
A.J. Horak
J.G.R. Horne
A.J.M. Horton
Geoff & Nadia Howes
Craig and Claerwen Howie
A.M. Hrywniak
John Huber
Neil Hulett
David Rex Hull
John Trevor Hund
Howard Hunter
I.A. Hunter
Ian B. Huntley
Kit Hustler
Neil Hustler
A.C. Hutchinson
A.R. Hutchinson
Doug & Jane Hutson
Tim Ivins
Philip Jack
Neels & Sandra Jacobs
R. Jagger
C.H.J. Janssen Schmidt
R. Jeffery
G.A. Johannes
E.R. Johannesson
Anthony Johnson
Clive Scott Johnson
Craig Denis Johnson
Ernest Johnson
Nigel Johnston-Stewart
W.P. Johnstone
A.T. Jones
Miss H.C. Jones
Linda Jones
Magnus & Marge Jooste
Sharon Joss
Dr & Mrs J.M.L. Joubert
Paul A.M. Joubert
Quintus Joubert
J.S. Gericke Library, University of
  Stellenbosch
Gwen & Claude Jugmans
David Kahn
Hillel M. Kahn
Sidney H. Kahn
B. & D. Kalshauen
Mark Kaplan
Mike & Leigh Kay
Clive & Aliki Kelly
Les Kennedy
Julius Kieser
H.W. Kinsey
J.J. Kirkness
Pamela Klapwijk
Timothy-Luke Klapwijk
D. Klein
A.J. & A.G. Klemptner
F.O. Klipp
Len Klodniski
Johan Kloppers
Bill & Heleen Knezovich
Nora Kreher
Carien Kretzschmar
Liezel Kretzschmar
J.A. du P. Kriek
J.J. Krüger
N.A. Kruger
Chris Labuschagne
Neil & Lesley la Croix
Paul A. Laesecke
G.M. Landmark
Geoff Lane
I.R. Lang
P. Langenhoven
Howard Langley
Herb, Rene & John Larkan
Phillip F. Lategan
P.J. Latham
Rev. E.H. Latsky
Cyril Laubscher
Brett Lawson
M. & J. le Roux
R. & E.E. le Roux
Charles & Bev Leach
S. & G. Ledger
Jackie Leech
John Lennard
P.J. du Pré le Roux
Letaba Arts and Crafts
R.E. Levitt
N.A.L. Lexander
Edward B.L. Lightbody
M.A. Lindeque
Donald Lindsay
Lionel Lindsay
Ian Hamilton Little
Lynton & Iris Lockwood-Hall
Henk & André Loots
F.J. Lordan
Olive & Peter Loubser
Anna & Albertus Louw
Koos & Hyla Louw
Peter J. Louw
At & Julene Lubbe
Desmond Lund
Mabula Game Reserve
Alastair & Margie MacDuff

Ian MacFadyen
Neville W. Mackay
Ian Mackenzie
Cally Mail
Danie Malan
Sharon & Francois Malan
Christian Manciot
J.H. & Malkah Mandelberg
Jack B.H. Manfield
N. Mankowitz
John & Bev Manning
Bob Manthé
André & Ann Marais
Prof. J.L.C. Marais
Paul Marchand
Henk Maree
Gerhard & Rykie Maritz
Michael Patrick Marriott
John Holroyd Martin
Rowan Martin
G.B. Maughan Brown
P.G. Mavros
Mbulwa Estate Limited
George McAllister
Stuart McArthur
Bruce & Margaret McBride
Ian McCall
D.A. Mc Carthy
Andrew McDonald
Kevin & Loreen McDonald
Ron McDonald
D.L. Mc Dougall
Peter O. McDougall
Jean McEwan
Bruce McIntosh
Bruce McLaren
Mr & Mrs I.R. Mc Nair
Daphne Mc Queen
Angus Meikle
F. Meischke
T.C. Menné
Menno & Krysia
Raleigh Meredith
Roland Meyer
Andrew Middleton
Philip Middleton
Dr & Mrs J. Midgley
Prof. C.J. Mieny
Basil & Mavis Miles
Brian & Moira Mills
F.I. Mockford
Ben Mol
Roger & Bronwyn Molver
Michael Mongeon
Neil Montgomery
H.A.V. Moodie
Mr & Mrs F.A. Mooney
E.K. Moorcroft
S.L. Moorcroft
Andy Moore
Charles & Carole Moore
John & Lyn Moore
M.L. Morlion
Richard Mourant
Charles Muller
Dup Müller
John & Morné Muller
Muller/Wilmot
John & Daphne Mullins
Leigh & Peter Mumford
Elizabeth Mundell
Neil Munro
Gareth W. Murray
R.M. Murray
Wim Myburgh
Gert Naude
Ester C. Nawrotzki
G.L. Naylor
A.C. Neethling
J.H. Neethling
Peter & Anne Nelson
T.M. Newsome
M.E. Nightingale
Cherrie & George Nisbet
Patricia A. Nisbet
Patrick Niven
M.W. Noakes
Bambi & Gilly Notten
R.H. Nourse
Eric Eugene Nutt
Peter Oberem
Dr. Ing E.H. Kurt Oblander
Michael Fredrick O'Brien
Pat O'Brien
Colin Ogden
Adrian Ogilvie
Derrick & Peggy O'Hagan
A.M. Olivier
L.L. Oosthuizen
George D. Orphanides
William Orton
Beverley Oscroft
Othawa Library – Richard Booth
Cyril & Cora Ovens
Mike Overall
Rod & Duifie Owen
A. & D. Painter
Raymond Etienne Paroz
Elspeth Parry
Jeff & Bev Parsley
Timothy J. Partridge

Mrs H.M. Paterson
Alan F. Payne
John R. Payne
John R.D. Pearşe
G.P. Peatling
Graham S. Peddie
Jeanne Peens
John & Mary Penny
S.G. Penny
Dika Pentlewood
Peter Pentz
Ina & Tibor Penzes
Cliff & Syd Petersen
R.N. Petzer
Anthony Pickering
Mike Pienaar
Evangelos John Pitsiladi
Rosemarie Ploger
P. & A. Pohl
Ted Pollett
Prof. Dr A.D. Pont
J.W. Pont
George & Penny Poole
Don & Jean Porter & Annie
Fritz & Karin Potgieter
Rod & Al Potter
Sally & George Prentice
John & Sharron Pretorius
Dr Marius Pretorius
Quentin Pretorius
Mariette Primic
Hendrik J. Prinsloo
Renate & Joachim Prinsloo
O.W. Prozesky
Dr Jerzy Przybojewski
Dr P. J. Pullinger
George A. Quenet
Gail Ractliffe
Richard Rademan
Fred & Martie Ramsay
Jonathan & Jennifer Rands
Tim & Linda Rands
Colin & Claire Rattray
D.G. Rattray
M.L.P. Rattray
Don Ravenscroft
Patty & Bernard Ravnö
Mr & Mrs A.A. Ray
Tim & Audrey Ray
Nic & Andrea Reay
Anita Redelinghuys
Dallas Reed
Paul & Theronia Reed
Peter Reeves
Josef H. Reichhof
Carlos Rein Duffau
W.A.C. Reniers
Dr H.J.J. Reynders
J.E. Reynolds
Paul & Barbara Reynolds
Andrew Richardson
T.W. Richmond
Dr Muriel B. Richter
I.M. Riddell
Elizabeth Rippon
Derek Christian Ritchie
R.B. Ritchie
Lynne Rivett-Carnac
Robbie Robberts
I.C. Robbie
Douglas Stuart Roberts
John Henry Roberts
David Robertson
T.R. Robson
Cedric Roche
Eva Roehl
Beryl Roest
Christian Rohleder
Dr G.F. Röhm
Bernhard Rolfes
Rose & Jill
John & Gill Rosmarin
Katherine & Kelly Ross
Robert & Marlia Rotteveel
Mrs Frances Rouse
A.A. Royston
Paul D. Rushworth
Gray Rutherford
Lawrence E. Ryan
Margriet & Hamid Sacranie
H. Sauer
Dudley Saville
Noel Saville
J.T.F. Schalkwijk
Ruth H.C. Schoeman
David Schreuder
E.W. Schroeder
Ruth A. Schroeder
Gaby Schultz
Albert Schultz
M.J.C. & I.C. Schweizer
Craig, Gareth & Andrew Schwikkard
Peter Mason Scott
Scottish Academy of Falconry &
  Related Studies
G.E. Scott-Ronaldson
R. Searle for Andrea & Marc Pienaar
Ron & Maureen Searle
Mark L. Segal
Selwyn & Wendy Selikowitz
Robert & Andrew Semple

Lorraine Shalekoff
Freddie, Miriam & Cinderella
  Shingange
Geoff Shorten
Peter-Stephen Shrimpton
H. Sibul
Gregg Sidman
Loren Sidman
Henry Jane & Erin Siebert
Lewis Silberbauer
Yochvud Silove
Willy, Wendy, Robert & Liza Simon
Ann C. Sinclair
Barry Sinclair
P.E. Skeat
Brian Slavin
Marc Sleen
Ernest Slome
Ansie & Dennis Slotow
Leon & Rochie Slotow
Rob Slotow
R.O. Small
C. Smeenk
B.E. & M.P. Smith
Elsa Smith
Jan Ryno Smith
Dr S.A. Smith
Dr S.A. Smith (Jnr)
Stephen G. Smith
B.W. Smorfitt
Michael & Morag Smuts
Jill & Mike Snaddon
Donald Sole
Donald & Silvia Spaidal
Mrs H.A. Spence
Kevin Spence
Derek William Spencer
Emile Sprenger de Rover
Ingwelala – Sprenger de Rover Family
Steven Squires
H.L. Stainthorpe
Richard & Barbara Stanley
S.A.H. Statham
Basil Stathoulis
Carol Stedall
David & Isolde Stegmann
R.J.L. Stein
D.Y. Stevens
J.Y. Stevens
Charles A. Stewart
Robert Stewart
D.P.J. Steyn
Johannes P. Steyn
John J.B. Steyn
Oscar W. Stopforth
Christopher & Carolle Stott
John G. Stowe
Nancy Stratten
Johann Strauss
B. & C. Street
John Stretton
Diana & David Stride
Johannes Strobos
Michel Stroud
Ian & Muriel Sturrock
Mark Sullivan
D.H.B. Sulter
Ian Sutherland
Eric Sutton
Wessel Swanepoel
C.M. Swarts
Mike Swartz
John & Lorraine Swinney
N.C. Symington
E. Taeuber
Takis Family
BruceTanchel
Carla Dayna Tanner
Peter V. Tarboton
G.F. & V.H. Taylor
Vincent & Pam Taylor
Dr Walter Thiede
Heinz Hermann Thiele
Joan W. Thorne
Jane & Colin Thorneycroft
Mrs R. Thorneycroft
Don & Westy Thring
Doug Throup
Caroline S. Tindall
Anthony David Tobin
Peter & Antonia Tolhurst
Marianna & John Tomazos
Peter & Noreen Tonkin
M.J.H. Tonking
Raymond J. Topp
Trevor & Annabel Townsend
G.K. Travlos
Neil Trollope
Dr M.R.B. Truscott
G.B. Truthe
Colleen Tucker (neé Bands)
R.B.K. Tucker
John & Jane Tumner
Garnett Twigg
Dr & Mrs J.C. Tyrrell
B.J. van Assen
Dr A.C. van Bruggen
Arsene van den Driessche
J.H. van der Byl
J.A.L. van der Colff
Pieter van der Hoven

Dick & Liz van der Jagt
Dr John Vandermade
S.W. van der Merwe
Wykert Robert van der Merwe
Paul & Gerda van der Reyden
Johan & Annatjie van der Sandt
Dr C.J. van der Schijff
Herman van der Schijff
Prof H.P. van der Schijff
L. Johann van der Schijff
Susan van der Schijff
Lisa van der Spuy
Johan van Eeden
B.J. van Heerden
Gerty van Heerden
Jeanette M. van Heerden
M.V. van Heerden
Elisabeth van Heesch
H. van Kerken
Dr K.M.A. van Laeren
Dr J. van Marle
J.J. van Niekerk
Laura A. van Niekerk
L.W. van Reenen
J.J van Rensburg
M. & M.A. van Rijswijck
Theo van Schaik
Manie & Maud van Straaten
Marius van Wyk
Helm van Zijl
Paul & Elsje van Zijl
Rawk van Zijl
Johan van Zyl
Nico van Zyl
Pieter W. van Zyl
Fanie & Julye-Ann Venter
J.M. Venter
Kirsten, Dirk & Karl, Venter
Dr Gerhard H. Verdoorn
Pieter & Nadine Vervoort
Graham & Milly Vickers
Kit & Hazel Vickery
J.G. Viera
Bernard K. Viljoen
Adele Vincent
Attie Visser
J.P. (Jannie) Visser
Etienne & Susann Vlok
Pieter & Nola Vlok
Willie & Joan Vlok
Dr & Mrs D.P. Voges
S.P. Voges
Eric von Glehn
Gert von Imhof
Carl-Henning von Ribbeck
Michael von Seidel
Dr & Mrs P. Vorster
A.J. Vos
Rex & Ethne Wakely-Smith
Brian Walker
Dave Walker
Jack M. Wall
A. Walsh
Terry Walton
Eric Warner
Prof. Ian B. Watt
Michael C. Watt
W.M. Wedderburn
Danie & Gerda Welman
John Welton
Johan Wentzel
J.B. Wessels
John Wesson
The Hon. Louis Weyers
Gill Wheeler
F.C.D. White
Tom Whiteway
J.W. Whittaker
L.J. Whyle
K.D. Wienand
David Wigley
Peter M. Williams
Jeremy W. Williamson
Nigel Willis
Jason L. Wilson
Molly Ann Wilson
Graham Wiltshire
John Winter
Robert & Bobbie Wise
Dr Geo. S. Withinshaw
Hilda & Jurgen Witt
Wessel Witthuhn
Trevor & Cheryl Wolf
Sherianne Wolman
Jamie & Stefan Woloszyn
B. Nigel Wolstenholme
Lyle S. Wood
E.J. Woodcock
G.W. Woodland
Charles D. Woodward
Mark Woolley
E.A. Wrangle
Rita Wright
Charles Wykeham
Mrs A.S. Wyrley-Birch
Yellowwood Park Primary School
Harry Yiannakis
Paul & Sue Yiannakis
Jake & Heather Yule
Michael Ziegler